AUSTRALIA'S
ORIGINAL
LANGUAGES

Books on linguistics by R. M. W. Dixon

Linguistic Science and Logic
What is Language? A New Approach to Linguistic Description
The Dyirbal Language of North Queensland
A Grammar of Yidiñ
The Languages of Australia
Where Have All the Adjectives Gone? And Other Essays in Semantics and Syntax
Searching for Aboriginal Languages: Memoirs of a field worker
A Grammar of Boumaa Fijian
A New Approach to English Grammar, on Semantic Principles
Words of Our Country: Stories, place names and vocabulary in Yidiny
Ergativity
The Rise and Fall of Languages
Australian Languages: Their nature and development
The Jarawara Language of Southern Amazonia
A Semantic Approach to English Grammar
Basic Linguistic Theory, Vol. 1, *Methodology*
Basic Linguistic Theory, Vol. 2, *Grammatical Topics*
Basic Linguistic Theory, Vol. 3, *Further Grammatical Topics*
I am a Linguist
Making New Words: Morphological derivation in English
Edible Gender, Mother-in-law Style and Other Grammatical Wonders: Studies in Dyirbal,
Yidiñ and Warrgamay
Are Some Languages Better than Others?
'We Used to Eat People': Revelations of a Fiji Islands traditional village
The Unmasking of English Dictionaries

with Alexandra Y. Aikhenvald
Language at Large: Essays on syntax and semantics

with Barry J. Blake (editors)
Handbook of Australian Languages, Vols 1–5

with Martin Duwell (editors)
The Honey Ant Men's Love Song, and Other Aboriginal Song Poems
Little Eva at Moonlight Creek: Further Aboriginal song poems

with Grace Koch
Dyirbal Song Poetry: The oral literature of an Australian rainforest people

with Bruce Moore, W.S. Ramson and Mandy Thomas
Australian Aboriginal Words in English: Their origin and meaning

For a full list of publications please go to
www.jcu.edu.au/lcrc/people/deputy-director

R. M. W. DIXON

AUSTRALIA'S ORIGINAL LANGUAGES

AN INTRODUCTION

ALLEN&UNWIN
SYDNEY·MELBOURNE·AUCKLAND·LONDON

First published in 2019

Allen & Unwin
83 Alexander Street
Crows Nest NSW 2065
Australia
Phone: (61 2) 8425 0100
Email: info@allenandunwin.com
Web: www.allenandunwin.com

A catalogue record for this
book is available from the
National Library of Australia

ISBN 978 1 76087 523 7

Set in 13/18 pt Garamond Premier Pro by Bookhouse, Sydney
Printed and bound in Australia by Pegasus Media & Logistics

10 9

The paper in this book is FSC® certified.
FSC® promotes environmentally responsible,
socially beneficial and economically viable
management of the world's forests.

Contents

Foreword

There has for some time been the need for a book for the general public on the nature of the Indigenous languages of Australia, their subtle grammatical structures and specialised vocabulary. Of how the languages reflect traditional values, and how culture determines the make-up of the grammar. And the ways in which they differ from the familiar languages of Europe.

This book, by Professor R. M. W. Dixon, meets that need. Bob Dixon came out from England, in 1963, to learn and study languages still spoken by members of the First Nations. He found that the original inhabitants were, at that time, not regarded as citizens; they were not permitted to live freely nor to operate their own bank accounts. There was scant understanding among mainstream Australians of their systems of social organisation and values; the later arrivals to the continent interwove arrogance with ignorance. The situation did gradually improve and, in the 1970s, Bob was able to assist his Indigenous friends in their quest for land rights. But there lingers a lack of understanding of the rich tapestry of the original languages, a lack which this volume seeks to satisfy.

For his general survey volume *Australian Languages: Their nature and development* (2002), Bob studied materials available for each of the 250 original languages of the continent. In the present volume, he quotes from more than three dozen separate languages. Speakers of Dyirbal adopted Bob into their community, sharing with him age-old cultural beliefs, and an intimate knowledge of the rainforest environment in which they live. Throughout the book, he draws extensively on this, his area of special expertise.

Bob Dixon has an international reputation for his work on general linguistics, including studies on the grammar of English and his three-volume magnum opus *Basic Linguistic Theory*. He has provided comprehensive documentation for Jarawara, spoken in the Amazonian jungle of Brazil, and for the dialect of Fijian spoken on the island of Taveuni. But his overarching interest and efforts have always been focused on Australian languages. Responding to the wishes of his teachers, the last fluent speakers, Bob has published grammars and vocabularies of five Indigenous Australian languages, plus collections of traditional legends and stories, and one volume of song poetry. All but one of these languages are no longer actively spoken but there are programs to revive them, in which Bob is enthusiastically participating.

I am honoured to introduce this volume, the outcome of half a century of immersion in the cultures and languages of the first peoples of Australia.

Alexandra Y. Aikhenvald
Distinguished Professor and Australian Laureate Fellow
James Cook University

1

Many distinct languages

The discovery and settlement of Australia took place at least 50,000 years ago. The immigrants soon spread out over the continent and split into many separate groups, which have been traditionally called 'tribes'. But each had its own country, its own political system and laws, and its own language and legends, just like the nations of Europe (albeit on a smaller scale). It is indeed appropriate to refer to them as 'nations', the First Nations of Australia.

These original inhabitants of Australia, the First Nations, were an enigma to the Europeans who came to share the land with them. Their unfamiliar outward appearance hid a multifaceted social organisation, a classificatory kinship system in which everyone is related to everyone else, and whose roles clearly define ritual responsibilities.

Nothing is more fascinating than the nature of the original languages. There are systems of cases on nouns and tenses on verbs more intricate than those in Greek and Latin. A distinctive speech style which must be used, as a mark of deference, between mother-in-law and son-in-law. A special gender for 'edible vegetables', to go alongside 'feminine' and 'masculine'. Song styles with distinctive metre and meaning. A plentiful vocabulary dealing with subtle distinctions for propensities such as generosity, jealousy, shame, and bravery.

A portrait of the rich texture of these original languages is presented in this volume. However, we need to start at the beginning, examining the attitudes and happenings which led up to the present-day situation for members of the First Nations and their languages.

In today's world, racism is something which right-minded people make an effort to avoid. Not everyone is, or ought to be, the same. We should respect other people's habits, customs, and religions, just as we expect them to respect those which we practise. Racism or lack of racism is basically an attitude. It is also a matter of recognition. If someone decides that a ritual which they witness in a foreign country is just a load of childish mumbo-jumbo, then they have no chance of appreciating its cultural significance, and of realising that it is perhaps as important and comforting for its practitioners as is Mass for members of the Roman Catholic church.

One of the strongest—but least recognised—expressions of racism is to denigrate another's language. In its strongest form this involves suggesting that a certain ethnic group doesn't really have a proper language, which could be put alongside Portuguese, or Welsh, or Latvian.

In 'Unpleasantness at Budleigh Court', a short story by P.G. Wodehouse, pellets from an air-gun impact on the posterior of famed explorer Colonel Sir Francis Pashley-Drake while he is sunbathing on the roof of the boathouse.

A sharp agonizing twinge caused him to break off abruptly. He sprang to his feet and began to address the surrounding landscape passionately in one of the lesser-known dialects of the Congo basin.

While familiar nations speak 'languages', ethnic groups in other parts of the world are held to communicate just through 'dialects'. In fact there are several hundred distinct languages spoken across the Congo Basin, as different from each other as Greek is from Italian, or Finnish from Swedish, and equally rich in grammar and vocabulary.

Saying that the modes of speech of the non-white inhabitants of Africa, or of Australia, or wherever, are just 'dialects' and declining to accord them the label 'languages' is instant degradation. It implies that they are limited, impoverished, the mark of an inferior people. This is simply untrue.

A language is a means of communication shared by the members of a community, or of several communities. The basic criterion for 'what is a language' involves intelligibility. If Jack can understand the mode of speaking of Jill and vice versa, then they are speaking forms of a single language. For example, Jack may be from Chicago and Jill from Liverpool; they use dialects of the English language. But if Jill is from Madrid and Jack from Amsterdam then they will be speaking two distinct languages, Spanish and Dutch, and will not be able to understand each other.

There are 120 or so languages spoken by about 740 million people across the 10 million square kilometres of Europe. Every one of them is of considerable intricacy (so that it takes real application to learn a new language as an adult). They range in size: Ingrian, spoken on the southern shore of the Gulf of Finland, is said to have only about 120 speakers, whereas Turkish has about 60 million and German 100 million or more. Each has roughly equal complexity: grammatical constructions and rules that take several hundred pages to enunciate, plus a vocabulary of a good few thousand words.

One can see how different the languages are by examining how to say 'This dog ran' in a sample of three:

POLISH	Ten pies biegł
ESTONIAN	See koer jooksis
ITALIAN	Questo cane corse
	This dog ran

In each sentence, the demonstrative 'this' comes first, then the singular form of the noun 'dog', and then a past tense form of the verb 'run' (however, word order can be varied, to some extent). In Polish and Italian 'dog' is of masculine gender, so that *ten* 'this' and *questo* 'this' are masculine singular nominative forms. Estonian has no gender system in its grammar; *see* is the singular nominative form of 'this'.

The population of Australia is estimated to have been between one and one and a half million before the intrusion of Europeans at the end of the eighteenth century. These people were spread across the seven and a half million square kilometres of the continent and spoke approximately 250 distinct languages, each as different from the others as are Polish, Estonian, and Italian. Some languages would have had just a few hundred speakers, others several thousand. Every one of these original languages of Australia has a sophisticated system of grammar and a vocabulary consisting of thousands of words. They are absolutely comparable in complexity to the languages of Europe or Asia.

The differences between the languages can be illustrated by seeing how to say the same sentence, 'This dog ran', in a sample of three:

DYIRBAL (around Tully, Qld)	Giñan guda jinggaliñu
BANDJALANG (around the Clarence River, NSW)	Gala dabaay gawarini
MARTUTHUNIRA (from the Pilbara region, WA)	Nhiyu muyi wanyjarrilha

This dog ran

As with the Polish, Estonian, and Italian examples, in each of these three sentences the demonstrative 'this' comes first, then the noun 'dog', and finally a form of the verb 'run', referring to past time. However, the order of words can be varied, especially in Dyirbal where they may be arranged in virtually any order.

Dyirbal has four genders: the first covers human males and most animals, the second includes human females and a few animals, the third edible plants, with the fourth being a residue set (full details are in chapter 9). *Guda* 'dog' is placed in the same gender as females (as it is in Russian), this being shown by the final -*n* of *giñan* 'this'. In Bandjalang *gala* 'this' refers to something which is visible, near the speaker, and of singular (rather than plural) number. Martuthunira has a system of three grammatical number values: singular, referring to 'one', dual for 'two', and plural for 'more than two'. *Nhiyu* is the nominative singular for 'this, near speaker' (dual would be *nhiiyarra* and plural *nhiingara*). Dyirbal, Bandjalang, and Martuthunira are distinct languages, and each has a number of dialects.

The word 'dialect' is used in two ways. The first is to describe a geographical variety of a language. The English language includes British, American, and Australian dialects. Each has characteristic features of pronunciation, word forms, word meanings, and grammar, but the dialects are mutually intelligible showing that they make up a single language. In like fashion, there are dialectal varieties of Polish, Estonian, and Italian, and also of Dyirbal, Bandjalang, and Martuthunira. This is the scientific use of 'dialect'.

The other sense is meant to be derogatory. When Colonel Sir Francis Pashley-Drake was said to be familiar with 'one of the lesser-known dialects of the Congo basin', the implication was that this mode of speech lacked the expressive power, or the refined structure, of the major languages of Europe. It was something less than a language, an inferior thing.

This is how the original languages of Australia are typically portrayed. An acquaintance calls me up and asks 'What was the word for "dog" in the Aboriginal dialect of Canberra?' I patiently explain that there were about 250 distinct Indigenous *languages* spoken across Australia—'languages' rather than 'dialects'—and that there was one *language* spoken around Canberra. The caller listens impatiently. 'Alright,' they say, 'but what was the word for "dog" in the Canberra dialect?' I've explained this umpteen times— to individuals, to groups, on the radio, on TV—and so have many linguistic colleagues.

But it never seems to sink in. Even higher-echelon media won't accord to the original population of Australia anything more than 'dialects', the term being used in its demeaning sense. The Labor party was elected to power in 1972, after 23 years of right-wing rule, and lost no time in announcing that children living in traditional communities would for the first time be taught in their own languages. The government said 'languages'. But the banner headline in the *Sydney Morning Herald* reporting this was: 'ABORIGINAL CHILDREN TO KEEP OWN DIALECTS'.

The Indigenous population of Australia was concentrated around the coasts and major rivers, where food resources were plentiful, although there were scattered groups across arid regions. The concentration of languages follows a similar pattern. One tongue, called the Western Desert language, was spoken (in quite a number of geographical varieties, or dialects) across parts of South Australia, the Northern Territory, and Western Australia, totalling about a million and a quarter square kilometres (about one-sixth of the continent). Languages spoken in a rainforest region would need far less territory to sustain their speakers.

As a further illustration of differences between languages, the box shows words for a domesticated dingo (the native Australian dog), later extended to cover the European dog, in the languages spoken around what are now capital cities:

language	spoken around	'tame dingo, European dog'
YAGARRA	Brisbane	miri
DHARUK	Sydney	din.gu
WUYWURRUNG	Melbourne	yirrangin
GAURNA	Adelaide	kadli
NYUNGAR	Perth	turta
NGUNAWAL	Canberra	mirigañ
LARAKIA	Darwin	mamarul

English has taken many names for Australian animals and plants from the original languages, a fair proportion coming from Dharuk, the language spoken around the first settlement, in 1788, at Sydney Cove. In Dharuk, a domesticated dingo was called *din.gu* and a wild dingo was *warrigal* (this word has also been borrowed into English as an alternative name for dingo).

Why is there no entry for the language spoken around Hobart in the list just given? Archaeologists tell us that the dingo was only introduced into Australia about 4,000 years ago. The land connection between Tasmania and the mainland was submerged around 7,000 years earlier. There were thus no dingos in Tasmania.

There is another way people have for referring to the ways of speaking of the first inhabitants of Australia. They talk of 'the Aboriginal language', as if there were just one. I receive a call from the assistant to a prominent politician. The minister has just bought a house called Maguy and he wants to know what this means in 'the Aboriginal language'. I explain—for the how-many-th time—that there were originally about 250 languages (only some of which have been fully documented), each with thousands of words. The caller persists: the minister requires an answer to his question, and won't have a very good impression of professors of linguistics if I can't supply it. (I don't get much of an impression of ministers and their assistants.)

Every culture has its particular formulas for greeting, and to accompany giving and receiving. 'Hello' and 'goodbye', 'please' and 'thank you' are important features of social interaction for languages from Europe and for some languages from other parts of the world. But by no means for all (in fact, not for the majority of languages worldwide). A statement such as 'This dog ran' is translatable into every language, but speech formulas are culture-specific.

Communication involves not just the bare forms of words but also the ways in which sentences are pronounced, together with facial expressions and bodily gestures. When an English speaker says *Please help me carry this heavy basket!*, inserting *please* is a indication that it is a request rather than a command. When speaking an Australian language, the same effect would be obtained by employing a gentle and friendly intonation. And instead of saying *Thank you*, a nod and a smile will convey the same effect. Or else the recipient may say 'I am happy now'.

When Jumbulu arrives at a camp, he may say 'I've arrived' and the people there can respond with 'You've arrived'. This is a bit more informative that the formulaic *Hello* (which is of unknown etymology). When leaving, he can say either 'I'm going, you stay!' or 'I'm leaving you', and the people in the camp will respond 'You go!'

This is instead of our *Goodbye* (which is a contraction of *God be with you!*, although many present-day speakers of English are unlikely to be aware of this). Speakers of all languages—in Australia, and right across the world—have socially appropriate ways of interacting, and they often convey more than our *please* and *goodbye*.

We can now examine dialects, using the term in its scientific sense, as a geographical variety of a language.

2

Each language has several dialects

Few languages are entirely homogeneous. There are likely to be differences of pronunciation, vocabulary, and grammar depending on the age of speakers, on where they live, and often also on occupation and social role.

People across all regions of Britain, America, and Australia acknowledge that they speak English, and they have little difficulty in understanding each other. But the manner in which they speak differs in small ways depending on where they live (or where they were brought up). Speakers of dialects in Scotland and parts of the USA pronounce the *r* after a vowel in words such as *bar* and *barn*; those from other dialect regions do not do so. There is a difference: the *r* is a rolled sound in Scotland but generally a smooth sound in America (similar to the way *r* is pronounced at the beginning of a word in English and Australian dialects, as in *red* and *road*).

One reads that there were originally at least 700 tribal groups in Australia. How does this square up with 250 distinct languages? It's quite simple: several tribes would speak mutually intelligible dialects of a single language, just as the UK, the USA, Australia, and New Zealand speak mutually intelligible dialects of English.

Fifteen dialect groups comprise the Western Desert language, spoken over a million and a quarter square kilometres of arid country. There are minor dialectal differences but the level of intelligibility between people in geographically dispersed centres is high, justifying the recognition of a single language.

The Dyirbal language was spoken in the rich rainforest of northeast Queensland, between the Great Dividing Range and the Coral Sea. Working from 1963 until 2002, I was able to document five dialects. The grammar is very similar across dialects, and most lexical words are identical. Here is a selection of words which do vary. The dialects are given in roughly north (Ngajan) to south (Girramay) order:

dialects in roughly north to south order	nape of neck	mouth	scrub turkey	water	black bean
NGAJAN (Russell River)	waju				
WARI (North Johnstone River)		jawa	mungarra	bana	gañjuu
MAMU (South Johnstone River)	dara				mirrañ
JIRRBAL (Tully River)		ngan.gu	guyjarri		
GIRRAMAY (Murray River)				gamu	gañjur

For the first four words in the table, one or more dialects in a northern block have the same form, with a different one in a southern block. Names for 'black bean (*Castanospermum australe*)', one of the staple foodstuffs, are particularly interesting. It is likely that the form now found in Girramay, *gañjur*, was originally in use across all dialects but has been replaced by *mirrañ* in Mamu and Jirrbal, two central dialects. In the northern dialects Ngajan and Wari, the final -*ur* has been replaced by a long vowel -*uu*, giving *gañjuu*. In fact the replacement of vowel-plus-*r* by the corresponding long vowel is a regular phonetic change in the two northern dialects. Other examples of it are:

	black goanna (*Varanus varius*)	hungry for vegetable food	armpit
NGAJAN and WARI	gugaa	ngamii	ngamuu
other dialects	gugar	ngamir	ngamur

The varieties of English spoken in America and Britain have similar vocabulary. But there are a few interesting differences; for example:

- When someone from Britain announced that they would be going around the lakes in a **caravan** for their summer holidays, an American listener was puzzled and could only think of a string of camels in the desert. The corresponding American term is **trailer** or **mobile home**.
- An American security official saw something odd-looking in the X-ray of my backpack. He was flabbergasted when I explained that it was just a **torch**, probably having an image of an oxy-acetylene welding tool. Then a more worldly colleague leant over and explained: 'That's what they call a **flashlight**.'
- A detective story set in Wales mentioned a body in the **boot** of a car. An American reader expostulated: 'Boots are for people,

automobiles have wheels.' The American term is **trunk**, which in Britain refers to a large, strong box with a hinged lid, for transporting things. A trunk can be placed in the boot of a car, if the boot is big enough.

- An American visitor to Britain, noticing many columns of people waiting patiently for buses, wrote back home: '**Standing in line** is so much a habit here that they even have a special term for it, a **queue**.'

A well-established word may have its meaning extended in different ways in diverse dialects. *Table*, as a noun, goes back to *tabule* in Old English. It came to be used also as a verb in modern times, after dialects had begun to diverge. A passage from Winston Churchill's history of the Second World War, from early 1942, goes as follows:

> The enjoyment of a common language was of course a supreme advantage in all British and American discussions . . . There were however differences of expression, which in the early days led to an amusing incident. The British staff prepared a paper which they wished to raise as a matter of urgency, and informed their American colleagues that they wished to 'table it'. To the American staff 'tabling' a paper meant putting it away in a drawer and forgetting it. A long and even acrimonious argument ensued before both parties realised that they were agreed on the merits and wanted the same thing.

Such dialectal differences were minor, and didn't hinder the Americans and British from collaborating to win the war.

When Europeans moved into the land of Dyirbal-speakers, from the 1860s on, they adopted into English some words from the Indigenous language. For example, a brown-and-white perching bird *Orthonyx spaldingii* was called *chowchilla*, an anglicisation of the Dyirbal name *jawujala*.

And of course there were borrowings in the opposite direction. The English term *motor car* became *mudiga* in Girramay and Jirrbal, but *mudaga* in northern dialects. Then there was a new kind of event, a person being knocked down and run over by a motor car. An established verb had its meaning extended to describe this eventuality, but the dialects varied as to which verb was used:

- The verb *dumban* means 'smash into and knock over', or 'pick up and take on the way'. For example, 'I bumped into her by mistake and knocked her over' and 'A flood washed away the camp'. In the Mamu dialect it was extended to 'run over'; this describes how a vehicle may hit a person or animal and carry them along with it.
- In the Jirrbal dialect, *daliñu* means 'smash into the ground' (for example, He bashed the stone on the ground, to break it into pieces) or 'fall on someone', and is the verb used for 'run over'. The focus here is how the vehicle simply spreadeagles a person or animal onto the ground.
- *Dadin* is a verb (in all dialects) meaning 'cover over'. For example: a cloud covers the sun, sit down on something, cover a cooking frame with bark to keep the smoke in when preparing a feast of eels. Just in the Wari dialect it is extended to 'run over', indicating that when a vehicle hits a person or animal they often finish up beneath it.

A vehicle running over someone or something can have a variety of effects. It may carry the victim along with it, it may just knock them flat, or they may be trapped under it. The verb extensions in the three Dyirbal dialects each focuses on one of the effects.

There are likely to be some minor differences of grammar between dialects, generally rather fewer than differences of vocabulary. For instance, an American will say: *Let's go eat.* This would not be possible for someone from Britain or Australia; they would have to say *Let's go to eat*, or *Let's go and eat.*

Dyirbal has a richer word structure than English. There are a number of affixes in English, such as prefix *un-* in words like *un-tie* and *un-clean*, and suffix *-ness* in *kind-ness* and *sad-ness*. But Dyirbal has more, often employing affixes where English would use prepositions. The idea of accompaniment is expressed in English by *with* and in Dyirbal by a suffix which is *-ba* in northern and *-bila* in southern dialects. For example (where *gajin* is 'girl' and the 'accompanying' suffix *-ba* or *-bila* is added to *guda* 'dog'):

NGAJAN, WARI, and MAMU dialects	Giñan gajin jinggaliñu guda-ba
JIRRBAL and GIRRAMAY dialects	Giñan gajin jinggaliñu guda-bila

This girl ran with a dog

The difference is small and people would be attuned to such dialectal variations (just as English speakers are aware that *tomato* is pronounced as /təmeitau/ in America but as /təma:tou/ in Britain and Australia).

If a language is spoken by a limited number of people all living in the same place, with constant communication between them, then it may be homogeneous, with no dialectal varieties. But as the population grows, groups of speakers will move off to other locations—over a river or mountain, across a bay, or even by boat to a far land. Different speech habits will develop in the several communities: manner of pronunciation, extending the meanings of words, maybe tabooing some words and creating new ones to take their place. Thus are dialects born. At first the differences will be minor. When people travel between places where the language is spoken, they will be able to understand each other, showing that these are indeed dialects of a single language.

As time goes by, linguistic differences will enlarge such that communication between people from different locations becomes less straightforward. The dialects are diverging and becoming separate languages. When this happens, erstwhile dialect groups may constitute themselves as distinct nations, each with its own language.

People often ask whether in time British, American, and Australian English are likely to become so different as to be considered three languages, each not readily intelligible with the others. This might have happened if the conditions still prevailed under which America and Australia were colonised, sailing ships being the means of communication. But things have changed with steam ships, aeroplanes and especially the media—newspapers and magazines, films and TV, and now the internet. As a consequence of increasing global communication, American, Australian, and British dialects of English are, in point of fact, now moving closer together.

Australia is such a large land that there has been plenty of space for geographical dialects to evolve, and then to diverge and develop into separate languages. It is well established that the Indigenous people entered Australia—which was then part of one land mass with New Guinea—more than 50,000 years ago; they would soon have spread out across the whole continent. Since then there have been profound physical changes. Geographers believe that 20,000 years ago water resources would have been scarcer than now, supporting a smaller population. As water became more plentiful it would naturally have led to groups allowing their numbers to expand, with societies splitting and new languages evolving. (There is more on this in chapter 11.)

The next chapter explores the role of language in society, and how this is realised in Indigenous Australia.

3

Language doing its job

Language is a core element in the social fabric of every human society. It is used for recounting histories, enunciating laws and customs, expressing emotions, composing songs and stories. Language enables a group to act as a team—whether constructing a building or a boat, or enticing animals into a trap. It is language which provides each person with a sense of identity (their name), of belonging (their social group), and their role in the society (tinker, tailor, soldier, or sailor).

Language and culture go hand-in-hand, so that each can only be properly appreciated within the context of the other. A traveller who describes how 'they do things differently here from what we do back home' will explain less than one whose observations open fresh doors of understanding and insight.

We can commence with the mundane. Every person needs to drink and eat. Houses and settlements are necessarily placed close to a river or spring or well; water can readily be carried or piped. Food is more varied; in some societies it comes mostly from game animals and fish, in others mostly from vegetables (whether planted or growing naturally), and in many communities from a judicious mix of the two.

The original inhabitants of Australia would spear larger animals, capture birds and lizards, and catch fish with line and bait, or in stone traps, or by impaling them. Vegetable resources varied with the terrain. In arid regions they might centre on grass seeds and occasional fruits. In rainforest—along sections of the east coast—there were many plants with edible parts. Native plums and cherries could just be picked and eaten, in the right season. And there were a number of staple foods which required considerable preparation, such as the black bean, *Castanospermum australe*.

In Dyirbal country, a profusion of ripe pods from the tall black bean trees (called *mirrañ* in central dialects) fall to the ground around March. The pods—15 centimetres or more in length—are easily split, revealing three or four nuts each about the size of a chestnut. Children float the half-shells as play-boats on a stream. The nuts are baked, sliced, and soaked in running water; they would be poisonous when raw, or at any stage before the whole preparation is complete.

First, an earth oven is set up in a sandy place. A large fire is lit and, when burnt out, the ashes are raked off and a deepish hole dug. The black bean kernels are placed on a lining of leaves from the native banana. They are covered with tea-tree bark and sand, another fire being lit on top, and left for quite a few hours before being taken out and sliced.

In the absence of metal tools, a slicing implement is fashioned from the shell of a stripey forest snail called *gajiri* (*Xanthomelon pachystylum*). The empty shell is stuffed firmly with grass and ground on the edge of a sharp piece of stone, moistened with a little water so that it becomes thin enough to be split with a thumb nail, producing a sharp blade. The roasted beans must then be sliced very finely in order to make sure all toxin is leached out in the final stage. This involves placing the slices in an open-weave dilly-bag (something like a long colander) in the running water of a stream for two or maybe three days. The beans are then ready to be eaten, or else packed and buried underground as reserve supplies for later in the year.

Techniques of instruction vary. In industrialised societies children go to school and may be trained for a type of work quite different from that practised by their father or mother. In Indigenous Australian societies, training was 'on the job'. A child would accompany a parent in undertaking daily tasks. They would at first just watch, and then help, and learn by imitating.

For a complex task, such as making a traditional bark blanket, there could be a commentary, with a parent naming the materials used and processes involved. Remaining within Dyirbal culture, a fig tree called *magurra* (*Ficus variegata*) is cut down (verb *nudin*). Two incisions (verb *gunban*) are made right round the circumference of the trunk (*yumal*), a metre or so apart, joined by an incision along the trunk. The bark (*guga*) is then prised off (verb *guñjin*), then separated into two layers (verb *ginbin*), with the outer layer discarded and the inner one retained. During this process edges are struck (verb *jindan*) with a stone (*diban*) so that the layers come apart easily.

The sheet of bark is now stretched out (verb *dajun*), banged out all over, and soaked (verb *ngaban*) in water until it is soft and flexible. It is then draped (verb *wandan*) on a frame (*warrga*) over a fire and gently singed (verb *ngalman*). Taken off the frame (verb *bundin*), it is laid down and tapped (verb *jinin*) up and down all over with a stick (*yugu*) or axe-head (*barri*). It is then soaked and squeezed (verb *julman*) so that all the sap (*jalnggan*) comes out (verb *mayili*).

It is again singed over the fire, then soaked in water for a couple of days, taken out and allowed to become dry (adjective *ngarrala*). The grey layer on the blanket is then yanked off (verb *buñjan*), so that just the woolly part is left. The blanket is now ready for use, to keep you warm on cool nights. When shifting camp it is easy to roll up (verb *balban*) and carry around (verb *budin*).

For activities which require considerable skill, there is provision of special training. Before attempting to spear a moving wallaby, youths practise with a slightly easier target. For the Dyirbal, this involves a *gugandal*, which is a long length of bark, joined up and fashioned into a not-quite-circular wheel. It is hurled into the air by an initiated man and boys attempt to throw their spears through the moving target. This can be practised many times, as preparation for serious hunting, when there is a single chance to secure meat for the family supper.

Every type of society has its conventions for social interaction. When a stranger comes to visit an Indigenous community, they will never walk right up to it. The accepted behaviour is to halt some way off, where you are visible, and wait to be beckoned forward. It may be a few minutes or a few hours or even a couple of days before the invitation comes. Language reflects convention. Dyirbal has a verb *yilgan* 'go almost to a place but stop a little way short of it' to describe this behaviour.

Vocabulary reflects what happens in the world around and is flexible enough to describe new eventualities. Consider the two verbs in Dyirbal for 'cross over':

LANGUAGE DOING ITS JOB **23**

- *Mabin* has a matter-of-fact meaning, describing going from one side to the other of a path, railway line, or river. The person or animal crossing keeps their feet on the ground (or body in water).
- *Mabirañu* is used for crossing through the air—a possum jumps from tree to tree, or a bush fire jumps over a gap in foliage (such as a road). It is also used for an illness crossing from one person to another. Where we might say 'Jack caught a bad cold from Jill', this would be rendered in Dyirbal by 'A bad cold *mabirañu* (crossed) from Jill to Jack'. A further sense evolved in the context of the European incursion. George Watson (born about 1899) was brought up in the traditional way by his Mamu grandfather. The grandfather died and George went to work for a local settler, helping to fell the forest for cattle grazing. As he described it to me, George *mabirañu* (crossed) into a different world, that of the white man.

A major role of language is naming—not just of things but of individual people. My name is what I am, my identity as a person distinct from others. Nothing is more irksome than for it to be badly pronounced or written wrongly. Then there is the matter of where I belong: the place I come from, the one I live in now. And my role and position, be it plumber, cashier, foreman, major-general, deputy head teacher, or whatever.

In regions where infant mortality is high, a name may not be bestowed upon a child until it has survived to be about six months old (grieving is less painful in the absence of a name). Typically, in Australian societies, an individual may have several names, each relating to a totemic animal or plant associated with the clan they belong to. A new name is often conferred at initiation.

There are also names for stages in a life-cycle, most of which can be used for address and for reference. In Warlpiri, from Central Australia, both boys and girls are called *wida* 'child' in infancy. However, after about the age of three, the sexes are accorded different labels. A young girl is *nalali*, when pubescent she becomes *djabinba*, succeeded by *maraguda* when mature, *ganda* after having borne a child, and *milgari* following the menopause and into old age.

For males, the progression is:

- From about the age of three until twelve, when the rites for making him a man begin, he is *murgu* 'boy' (or *bubu-gari* 'with a foreskin').
- At about twelve, he leaves his mother's camp and goes into pre-circumcision seclusion, now being called *burunjungu* which is literally 'the hidden one'.
- He is then taken by initiated men on a grand tour of nearby communities and during this is called *malulu*.
- Next comes circumcision, the first stage of initiation, and after it the boy will be known as *juguru* (or *bubu-wangu* 'foreskin-lacking'). The juguru are taught about the manufacture and use of weapons, about hunting techniques, and essentials of the Indigenous religion.
- At about the age of sixteen (when his moustache is becoming noticeable) it is time for the second stage of initiation. This is subincision, which involves creating an opening at the base of the penis into the urethra (urinary duct). The youth is then a *bara-banda* 'he with a subincision wound' or 'fully initiated man' and will be such for the remainder of his life. There is further instruction from older men concerning origins, rituals, and life-skills; this is continuous over the next several decades.

- The newly initiated youth now goes to live with the other unmarried men, and is called *jambiwiri-wanu* 'he of the bachelors' camp'.
- Once the young man has proved himself to the satisfaction of his potential mother-in-law (and other key relatives), he may marry, this stage in the life-cycle being termed *jubugara* 'married man'.
- Twenty or so years later comes the stage of *ngarga* 'middle-aged'. He will by then have accumulated considerable knowledge, and attention will be paid to his opinions on important matters.
- And finally *bulga* 'old man', someone who has great wisdom but is failing physically, unable to hunt and fight as he used to.

Just about every human society delights in ceremonies. Universities are pretty relaxed places nowadays but parents do expect to see the professors amassed in gaudy robes smiling over young Robin as the certificate is ceremoniously handed over. There are coronations of kings and queens and inaugurations of presidents. Not for all, but for many, there is the wedding ceremony. Months may be spent in planning venue, feast, cake, and band. And of course finery for bride, bridesmaids, and bride's mother to wear.

The original Australians make no big deal over marriage. The couple will have been promised to each other some years before and when the time is considered appropriate they simply set up a conjugal camp. The Australians' ceremonies are initiation, and seasonal rituals, some performed by initiated men and some by women.

In a number of locations there is a special speech style which is taught to youths at initiation and may only be used by those who have undergone the rite. Among the Lardil nation on Mornington

Island, the initiation register uses exotic sounds such as clicks, similar to those in Zulu and other southern African languages. In one language from Central Australia the initiation register involves replacing a word by its opposite. If one initiated man says to another 'Someone else is standing', the actual meaning is 'I am sitting'.

All of humankind indulges in aesthetic creation—through art, dance, story, and song. The original inhabitants of Australia pursued a variety of genres. There would be love songs to assist in wooing. Songs describing everyday events—with an accompanying dance—for performance at inter-tribal corroborees. And song-cycles, with hundreds of individual poetic components, which would take several nights to perform right through. They told of the travels, experiences, and activities of Dreamtime ancestors, the tracks they took, and what befell them on the way. The whole religious creed served to explain the way in which places and creatures are today.

Songs generally have the same form as spoken poetry, typically characterised by metre and rhythm. And often also rhyme, a feature found in languages of Europe and the Middle East (but seldom in those from elsewhere). A common poetic form, the sonnet, has fourteen lines each of ten syllables made up of five iambic feet (an unstressed syllable followed by a stressed one); rhyme schemes vary. A limerick has five lines, the first, second, and fifth consist of three iambic feet and they rhyme; the third and fourth have two iambic feet and they also rhyme.

There are four main types of song poetry for speakers of Dyirbal, each with its own subject matter, instrumental accompaniment, social role, and metrical pattern. They can be grouped into pairs as 'corroboree songs' and 'love songs' (these labels were provided by bilingual speakers). In spoken language, each word is stressed on its initial syllable but the song styles show varying patterns.

I. Corroboree songs. A number of neighbouring groups meet together for a corroboree, where news might be exchanged, disputes settled, marriages arranged, and future plans discussed. Songs and accompanying dances are an essential feature.

The male singer stands, accompanying himself by clapping together two boomerangs each held at its middle. Several women— generally including his wife (or wives)—crouch nearby, each banging a skin drum stretched tight across her thighs. A number of men painted with white, yellow, and red clay, and with charcoal, dance and mime the event described. Most corroboree songs deal with an everyday topic: hunting Torres Strait pigeons, a white man being stung by hornets, a willy wagtail bird wiggling his tail as he dances shake-a-leg style, like a ghost in the spirit home.

There are two corroboree styles:

Ia. A **Marrga** song consists of four lines, each of eight syllables. The first two lines are alternated several times, there is an instrumental interlude, then the second pair of lines is alternated. Each word has an even number of syllables with the final word in each line being a verb in non-future inflection. Stress goes on the first, fourth, sixth, and eighth syllables of each line.

Ib. A **Gama** song has two lines, each of eleven syllables, repeated alternately many times. Each line has three parts:

—Part A: five syllables, the first and fourth bearing stress. Either one word of five syllables, or a disyllabic word followed by a trisyllabic one.
—Part B: a disyllabic word, stressed on the first syllable.
—Part C: a word of four syllables, with stress on the first and final syllables.

This can be illustrated with a song describing hunters sneaking up on a grazing kangaroo from the leeward side, so as not to be detected by the roo as it stands alert, scratching itself, and sniffing for danger. One dancer mimics the kangaroo, and the others the stealthy hunters.

Hunting a kangaroo—Dyirbal song in the Gama style

Banja	jabara	baga	jumala-gu
follow	sneak.up	spear	woomera-WITH

Follow him, sneak up and spear him, using a woomera

Nguñju	binbangu	yuri	duganangu
alert	scratching	kangaroo	sniffing

The kangaroo stands alert, scratching himself, sniffing

II. Love songs. These are sung by men or by women, at any time, either privately to one person or semi-publicly. Accompaniment is by tapping with a piece of lawyer cane called *baygal* (*Calamus radicalis*) on a specially prepared *gugulu* stick. This is made from a hard wood, preferably *jidu* (*Halfordia scleroxyla*), which is called in English saffron heart or jitta. The *gugulu* stick is about 50 centimetres long with an oval cross-section (about 5 centimetres by 2.5 centimetres) and a gentle point at one end, all surfaces rubbed smooth.

Gugulu songs (as they are often called) have a different kind of message and subject matter from corroboree songs, often conveying personal feelings, of love or jealousy or revenge, or personal discomfort, or happiness. For example, a pregnant woman craving a feed of brush-tail possum, a lament of unrequited love, marvelling at a brightly shining star. There are songs concerning white people, some expressing distress at how the Indigenous people have been treated, and their sacred sites desecrated.

There are two main Gugulu styles:

IIa. A **Jangala** song consists of any number of lines, each of six syllables, which are repeated in variable order for a considerable time. The words can have any number of syllables with each being stressed on its initial syllable, as in spoken language.

IIb. A **Burran** song has four lines, of six, three, six, and three syllables respectively, repeated in strict sequence a fair number of times. Each trisyllabic line is a single word. The six-syllable lines can only include words with an even number of syllables. Once again each word is stressed on the initial syllable, as in spoken language.

The arrival of Europeans brought novel activities, described by new words and sometimes celebrated in song. Fields of sugar cane (rendered by *juga*) are harvested and sent to be crushed at the mill (*miyil*) in the town of Mourilyan (*Mirili* in Dyirbal). The mill's horn blares out and Dyirbal people suggest that this is a signal of the mill craving for more cane to crush, a fit subject for a Burran song:

The mill wants more cane to crush—Dyirbal song in the Burran style

Wunggurr	binu	bilu
stuttering.noise	SONG.WORD	noise of horn

It is intermittently honking its horn

Mirili
Mourilyan

At Mourilyan

Walnggarrañu	miyil
worrying.for	mill

The mill is wanting, worrying

Juga-gu
sugar-FOR

For more sugar cane

Most words in songs are the same as in spoken language, but there is a scattering of 'song words', such as *binu* here, essentially created to maintain the poetic metre. (Some of these special words may recur in several songs, some apparently only in one.)

Other language communities in Australia have quite different styles of songs, always intricate in structure, rich in subject matter, and with a determined social role.

This chapter will have served to open a window into the nature of Australian languages—providing identity, description, the means for interaction, and a conduit for aesthetic release. Not all observers have appreciated this. The next chapter surveys past opinions, some uninformed and some perceptive.

4

Nothing primitive here

The first impression one gets of a person, or a place, or a group of people, is likely to stick, and be difficult to expunge. A foreigner happened to visit a certain city during the only really hot month the city had experienced in a decade, and later persisted in writing: 'How I envy you your lovely sunny weather'. If the visitor had only stayed around for a bit longer that impression would have been tempered by biting winds, rain, hail, and almost continuous cloud.

William Dampier was the first Englishman to encounter the original inhabitants of Australia (then called New Holland). His book *A New Voyage Round the World* became a bestseller when it was published in 1697.

Dampier had gone to sea as a boy and spent decades on pirate ships around the Americas, Africa, and Asia. With an ever-enquiring mind, he studied flora and fauna when on land, and tides and a typhoon when at sea. Dampier was on board the *Cygnet*, commanded by Captain Reed, when in January 1688 it put into what is now called the Dampier Peninsula, in north Western Australia. There he came into superficial contact with members of the Bardi nation, and wrote of them 'The inhabitants of this country are the miserablest people in the world'. The words were epigrammatic. A first impression. And it stuck.

From the little he saw, much was inferred. First, general disparagement: 'The inhabitants of this country are the miserablest people in the world . . . Setting aside their human shape, they differ but little from brutes.' There is physical description: 'great bottle-noses, pretty full lips, and wide mouths'. Then comments on ways of living: 'they have no sort of clothes . . . they have no houses . . . their only food is a small sort of fish, which they get by making weirs of stone across little coves or branches of the sea'. Finally: 'I did not perceive that they did worship anything'. (How could he possibly tell? And, in any case, is it a bad thing to be self-sufficient to the extent that one does not need to worship something?)

Dampier had encountered the Bardi in the monsoon season which they call *Mankal*, when fishing in weirs is important. This is also a good time for digging up turtle eggs, which he did not notice. If he had come a few months later, in the cold season called *Barrgon*, there would have been hunting of dugong (*odorr*) and a plentiful supply of fruits and vegetables. Later in the year, around November, came *Lalin*, the season for turtle hunting and the time for *iilarra*, wild apples (*Syzygium subordiculare*) to ripen.

The Bardi often slept in rock shelters (or caves), called *gardin*, or else erected *baali*, low huts made from pandanus or other palms. Like other peoples of Australia, they believed in a spirit world with ancestral creator beings, and performed many significant ceremonies. This could be called a 'religion' but it is entirely different from the deity-based practices familiar to Dampier.

Besides genital covers, they had no clothes and required none.

Dampier's attitude is instructive in this respect. He looked upon the Bardi nation as if they were a kind of debased and deprived Europeans. Having filled some barrels from wells of fresh water, these needed to be transferred to the ship.

> It being somewhat troublesome to carry to the canoes, we thought to have made these men to have carried it for us, and therefore we gave them some old clothes; to one an old pair of breeches, to another a ragged shirt, to the third a jacket that was scarce worth owning, which yet would have been very acceptable at some places where we had been, and so we thought they might have been with this people. We put them on them, thinking that this finery would have brought them to work heartily for us; and our water being filled in small long barrels . . . we brought these our new servants to the wells, and put a barrel on each of their shoulders for them to carry to the canoe.

The Bardi people could not be bought. They had no wish for clothes and discarded the tattered garments. They saw no reason to carry barrels for those who were too lazy to do it themselves. Dampier was wholly mistaken in thinking he could buy servants. The original inhabitants of Australia have a different view of the world, and of themselves, from that of the English. They do have a strong sense of obligation within their intricate system of kinship relationships. But they will not be beholden to outsiders.

Dampier had a rough-and-ready literary style, but he could convey a picture of exotic places never before described. *A New Voyage Round the World* became the talk of the town and brought him respect. Indeed, in 1699 the Admiralty gave Dampier command of HMS *Roebuck* for a voyage to explore New Holland. The ship put in to several places down the Western Australia coast, including the islands now referred to as the Dampier Archipelago. One of the nations living there was the Martuthunira, whose language was quoted in chapter 1.

Although the contact was even slighter than before, Dampier's opinion from eleven years earlier was confirmed. 'They all of them have the most unpleasant looks and the worst features of any people that ever I saw, though I have seen a great variety of savages.' A group of men attempted to repel the invaders using spears, one of which narrowly missed Dampier. 'I thought it high time to charge again and shoot one of them, which I did.'

He observed the Martuthunira eating shellfish and gratuitously assumed that this was their main foodstuff. On the contrary, they hunted dugong (*nyamina*) and turtle (*majun*), obtained whiskered salmon (*kanaranka*) and half a dozen other varieties of fish from the rivers. There was abundant vegetable food, such as mangrove nuts (*thuriyal*) and wild beans (*walyurru*). Also honey (*kunkuwarra*) from native bees, and much else.

Dampier's new book *A Voyage to New Holland*, published in 1703, reinforced the 'miserablest people' disparagement. It is interesting to enquire why this phrase should have resounded so loudly. There is no doubt that a part of the effect of this phrase results from Dampier's limited command of standard English. The superlative degree is expressed by suffix *-est* or by modifier *most*. Short words only take *-est* (*longest* rather than *most long*), a few may take either the suffix or the modifier (both *noblest* and *most noble* are used), and many longer words are confined to *most*. One says *most pleasurable*, rather than *pleasurablest*, *most forgettable* rather than *forgettablest*. And the preferred superlative form of *miserable* was in Dampier's time—as it is today—*most miserable*, not *miserablest*.

Dampier's literary sophistication was not great and he

over-extended the use of suffix *-est* in applying it to *miserable*. Had he said 'the most miserable people in the world' it would have resonated far less than 'the miserablest people in the world'. This non-standard use of *-est* added an almost poetic flavour to the phrase.

The 'miserablest people' description spread across the world and down through the years. French, Germans, Russians were led to believe—then and now—that the original inhabitants of Australia counted as lowest of the low. When I was at school in England, in the 1940s, we were told that Australian Aborigines were at the bottom of the hierarchy of civilised beings, just a rung or two above apes. (It was said, in contrast, that the Māori of New Zealand were near the top of the 'blackfellow ladder', only a short distance below Europeans.) When I went to university and read an account of the elaborate systems of nominal classification in languages from the Kimberley region of Western Australia, the Damperian dictum appeared unfounded. And then, when I was adopted into a First Nation community, and experienced the richness of culture and language, it became beyond nonsense.

From a European viewpoint, the material circumstances of these Australian peoples appeared to be decidedly limited. But if the Englishmen had stayed long enough to understand the languages, they would have been awed by their grammatical wealth. Whereas Latin, for instance, has a system of six cases on nouns, Bardi boasts of ten and Martuthunira more than a dozen. Similar complexities attend verbs and adjectives, pronouns and relative clauses. There was much more which went unseen. These tropical people had no need for clothes (other than small garments to maintain modesty) but required each member to pass through ceremonies as they ascended from one age-grade to another, rituals of greater moment than Anglican confirmation or Jewish bar mitzvah.

Judgement of any phenomenon can only be made from a particular perspective. Suppose that there are two stretches of river. The first is deep and clear with low flat banks. The second runs around boulders, with many rapids, and steep rocky banks. A merchant extols the first stretch as allowing easy passage for his cargo boats and a clear tow-path for barges. The second stretch is declared to be of no use whatsoever. A privileged gentleman, on the other hand, reaches an opposite opinion. The second stretch offers many waterholes for productive fishing and breathtaking views to photograph and paint. The first stretch is, for him, absolutely dull and without interest. Dampier is akin to the merchant; the original inhabitants of Australia have a viewpoint similar to that of the gentleman.

Following Dampier's lead, Australian peoples were referred to as 'primitive'. Before exploring what this is supposed to mean, it is instructive to look briefly at the second encounter of Englishmen with Australians, which took place on the other side of the continent.

In mid 1770, James Cook spent seven weeks ashore at what is now called Cooktown, in north-east Queensland, while his craft, HMS *Endeavour*, was repaired from damage sustained on the Great Barrier Reef. His interaction with the local Guugu Yimidhirr nation was generally cordial and showed a quite different attitude from that of Dampier. If there is no language in common, one can still exchange names. Cook's crew presumably offered their own names and the locals responded. They were introduced by name, 'a ceremony which, upon such occasions, was never omitted'. The Guugu Yimidhirr often came on board ship: 'We had another visit from four of the natives. Three of them had been with us before, but the fourth was a stranger whose name, as we learnt from his companions who introduced him, was Yaparico.'

One cannot imagine Dampier inviting local people aboard his ship, let alone offering to exchange names. Cook, Joseph Banks, and other members of the party elicited terms for body parts, birds, animals, and more (something Dampier never attempted). Cook generally behaved in an equitable way and the Guugu Yimidhirr expected him always to do so. One day the crew caught three large turtles. The locals suggested that one should be given to them (after all, it had been caught in their waters). This was absolutely refused and in retaliation the Guugu Yimidhirr set fire to long grass close to where some of the ship's goods were laid out. Cook then 'fired a musket charged with ball abreast of them' so that they departed. (Unlike Dampier, he did not fire *at* them.)

Cook was, of course, acquainted with Dampier's 'miserablest' dictum, but did not share his predecessor's blinkered perspective. He essayed a view from the other side of the fence:

> From what I have said of the Natives of New Holland, they may appear to some to be the most wretched people upon Earth, but in reality they are far more happier than we Europeans, being wholy unacquainted not only with the superfluous but the necessary Conveniences so much sought after in Europe, they are happy in not knowing the use of them. They live in a Tranquillity which is not disturbed by the Inequality of Condition: The Earth and sea of their own accord furnishes them with all things necessary for life, they covet not Magnificent Houses, Household-stuff &c, they live in a warm and fine Climate and enjoy a very wholesome Air, so that they have very little need of Clothing and this they seem to be fully sensible of, for many to whome we gave Cloth &c to, left it carelessly upon the Sea beach and in the woods as a thing they had no manner of use for. In short they seem'd to set no

NOTHING PRIMITIVE HERE **39**

Value upon any thing we gave them, nor would they ever part with any thing of their own for any one article we could offer them; this in my opinion argues that they think themselves provided with all the necessarys of Life and that they have no superfluities.

Each human being is a complex phenomenon, made up of many strands. There is the mental component: thinking, assessing, deciding. The social factor: relating to family, to an ethnic or national group, to sporting clubs and associations, and just to mates. Then the material part: wearing clothes, having a house to live in, plus cars, refrigerators, heaters, phones, computers, and all manner of other machines and gadgets.

Within each society, different people specialise in different ways. A philosopher may live alone with just a simple chair, a table, and a bed of boards, together with piles of books, pen, and paper. Someone with much money (whether inherited or amassed through astute dealings) may wallow in posh possessions but devote little time to reflection on the nature of life (hasn't any opinions, hasn't any ideas). A socialite will devote much effort to organising anything they can lay their hands on: family (both close and distant), church, political groups, charitable organisations, you name it.

All have something of every strand but each to a different extent. There are degrees of specialisation, in every direction. It is the same with nations and with ethnic groups. The peoples of Australia had a basic tool-kit. There were spears for hunting (and for fighting), plus woomeras (spear-throwers) which give a spear greater direction and force. Different varieties of boomerang were used for hunting, for musical accompaniment, and for play. Fish could be caught with multi-prong spears, with nets, with line and hook, in stone weirs, or by squeezing an anaesthetic vine over the water. Grinding-stones, winnowing dishes, bark bags for carrying water or honey, woven dilly-bags for a baby or foodstuffs. Stone axes, means for sharpening them, an apparatus for producing fire. Quite a number of other artefacts, including some of mystical significance for use in ceremonies, both secret and public.

Each group had its own territory and moved around it according to the season. The coastal group of Yidiñ-speakers, just south of the present city of Cairns, would travel up to the tablelands in the wet season—when the coastal flats were particularly hot, humid, and insect-ridden—to feast on yellow walnut, *ganggi* (*Beilschmiedia bancroftii*) and roasted *mudi*, lawyer cane (*Calamus moti*), which were in season there. And in the winter the tablelands group would come down to the coast for black walnut, *digil* (*Endiandra palmerstonii*) and silver quandong, *murrgan* (*Elaeocarpus angustifolius*), avoiding mountain frosts and mists.

Clothes are unnecessary—indeed, can be an impediment—in a warm climate. But in southern parts of Australia it can get cold and people wore cloaks made of possum skin. If a group moves around its territory according to when various fruits are ripe, or when fish and eels will be fat and plentiful, then a temporary shelter—which can be easily erected—is adequate. Dyirbal speakers lived in a region with the highest rainfall and they built more substantial and comfortable dwellings (called *yabun*) which people would return to each wet season for a number of years.

The machine-happy rich man may condemn the philosopher's life-style as frugal; but this scholar has all that he needs. In a similar way, Europeans denigrated the original people of Australia as 'primitive' in terms of their limited range of artefacts; however, they had what was needed for their way of life. And that was only one facet of Australian society. Others were highly developed: intricate kinship systems carrying a gamut of social responsibilities. And languages far more complex in their structure than most of the familiar tongues of Europe. These statements will be enlarged upon in following chapters.

Say all this to the person in the street and there is an overwhelming response: 'Oh, but they didn't have any writing system, did they?' It is said in triumph, as if it were something to which there could be no reply—no written language, therefore of no value. In fact, nothing could be less true.

Humankind evolved 120,000 years or more ago. Within a few thousand years, human languages would have evolved to something approaching their present level of complexity. (All languages spoken across the world today have an intricate structure. Despite some uninformed—and undoubtedly racist—opinion, no modern language could in any sense be called 'primitive'.) Language is first and foremost something to be spoken; a technique for writing it down is an optional extra. And writing systems developed quite late, no more than 5,000 years ago.

Literature doesn't need writing. Homer's magnificent epic poems, the *Odyssey* and the *Iliad*, were composed orally, before the introduction of writing into Greece. They were handed down by word of mouth, through generation after generation, before being eventually inscribed on parchment. There has been a written form of English for almost 1,500 years, but before the nineteenth century it was known to only a tiny fraction of the speech community. Even those who could write did so much less than they spoke.

A villager in mediaeval England did not need to write. Everything that should be known was remembered. (Once things come to be written, memory is relied upon less and tends to fall into attrition.)

There were folk tales which had been handed down through the ages, to be recounted around the fireplace in winter.

Writing systems (orthographies) have only been created a handful of times, and are then spread and borrowed as needed. Most groups in the Americas, Africa, Australia, the Pacific, and large parts of Asia only acquired orthographies when these were provided by missionaries, for the purpose of translating the Bible or some similar document. In the course of daily life, they were simply not needed. In summary, judging some group according to whether it has (and had) a writing system is a fake shibboleth.

In many societies there are stories recounting the beginnings of the world and how creatures and things came to be as they are. Australian nations had many detailed origin legends. Dreamtime ancestors created mountains, poured out water to fashion rivers. They painted birds into different colours. They extracted the poisonous fangs from pythons (who are now, as a result, harmless) but were unable to do the same for the taipan and the death adder (which are now among the most dangerous snakes in the world).

There is remarkable similarity between different cultures. The book of Genesis tells how Jehovah created the first man, Adam, from dust. Then he took a rib from Adam and made it into Eve, the first woman. A Dyirbal legend tells how a boil grew on the thigh (*ngaga*) of the first man. When it burst, the first child came out of it, a boy who was called Ngaga-ngunu ('thigh-OUT.OF'). The story of Adam and Eve was handed down orally for a thousand years or more until it was finally written. The story of Ngaga-ngunu would have been recounted through many generations (and then I helped write it down).

The first inhabitants of Australia had an intimate association with the land which harboured them. The characteristics and uses of each living creature and plant were learnt at an early age. Speakers of Dyirbal lived in dense rainforest country. During the 1980s there were just two scientists able to recognise and interpret every one of the more than a thousand distinct plants in this jungle. I worked with one of them, Tony Irvine, and a number of Dyirbal elders (the last generation who had full traditional knowledge). In all we identified almost 600 plants—names in one or more Dyirbal dialects, botanical name, and common name in English (if there is one).

For every distinct plant species recognised by western science there was a distinct Dyirbal name, and vice versa. The value of each tree or vine or shrub was noted. About 180 of the plants have edible parts. Some have timber suitable for constructing the frame of a house, others bear leaves used for thatching. Some are suitable for making shields, others for woomeras, or boomerangs, or sticks to dig up yams. The flowering stem of the grass tree, *birran* (*Xanthorrhoea johnsonii*), was ideal for the shaft of a spear, while the black palm, *gubungara* (*Archontophoenix alexandrae*), was preferred for the hard point on a spear (but if this was not available there were half a dozen acceptable alternatives).

Some trees had soft timber which would break easily, and were really of no use, but they were still all named. Others were central to the life of the community. One such was *jidu* (*Halfordia scleroxyla*); this is called in English saffron heart or jitta, the latter adapted from the Dyirbal name. The timber of *jidu* is hard and flexible, but not too heavy. It was used for swords, fish hooks, the peg on a woomera (into which the end of a spear fits), and the finely smoothed *gugulu* stick, used to accompany styles of 'love songs' (described at the end of chapter 3). If the end of a *jidu* stick was bashed down, this was ideal as a night-time torch, burning brightly and long. Also, the *jidu* tree bore fruit, much loved by cassowaries but not eaten by people.

There were a number of varieties of that remarkable artefact, the boomerang. The best known is the one which returns to the sender, and this was used for sport and amusement. More important was the heavier kind used for hunting and fighting, which did not return to the sender. It was intended to impact on the target, wounding or killing it. L.E. Threlkeld was the first missionary in Australia, living among the Awabakal nation near what is now the city of Newcastle in New South Wales. In 1826 he wrote:

> When thrown for the purpose of destruction, whether at man or beast, it is sent forward so as to strike one of its points upon the ground at some distance from the thrower, and the object intended to be hit, when the Boomerang rebounds, apparently with accelerated velocity, and strikes with astonishing force the victim, inflicting a most serious wound with the sharp edge of the weapon at the flat point. . . . It rips up the individual when it strikes, as though done with a knife, as I witnessed once in my own mare which was accidentally most seriously wounded by the Boomerang.

In territories with plenty of food and water resources, people would only have to move a short distance from one camp to another and it was possible to carry a fair range of implements. But people living in the central deserts roamed far in search of a new waterhole and were constrained as to how much they could carry. It was here that the boomerang came into its own. The hunting boomerang had a sharp hardwood edge which could be used as a knife. It was also utilised as a hammer, a club, a digging stick, and a percussion instrument for song accompaniment. And it could be used to make fire—rubbed to and fro at speed across a softwood surface, the sharp edge of the boomerang generates enough heat to cause a spark, lighting dry bark or grass.

The English word boomerang comes from *bumariñ*, the word for the hunting/fighting version in Dharuk, the language originally spoken around Sydney. Boomerangs were used all over Australia except in a few pockets mostly on the coast. The box shows varying names in a selection of languages.

language	spoken around	'boomerang'
BARDI	Dampier Peninsula	irrgili
MARTUTHUNIRA	Pilbara	wirra
GUUGU YIMIDHIRR	Cooktown	wangi
AWABAKAL	Newcastle	tarama
WUYWURRUNG	Melbourne	wan.gim
NGUNAWAL	Canberra	warungan
NYUNGAR	Perth	karli

In the English spoken in Western Australia, the boomerang is often called *kylie*, based on the word in Nyungar, and this has come to be used as a woman's name.

To summarise, a casual observer—such as Dampier—decided that the original inhabitants of Australia had few of the artefacts which he valued. Had he lived among them for a while, it would have become plain that there was available a wide variety of fish, meat, fruit, and vegetables, and a tool-kit which served all needs. If he had tried to become integrated into the society, it would have been necessary to master the kinship system, which is far more elaborate than anything within his English experience. (This will be explored in the next chapter.)

If an observer should persist in regarding the material side of life, for the original Australians, as being 'primitive', there is a tendency to propose a correlation: 'If they are a primitive people, they must speak a primitive language'. Not so, not in the slightest. People who do not over-exploit the material side of things tend to specialise in those other facets of humankind, the social and the mental. This last is channelled into the original languages, which are vehicles for detailed grammatical specification, for the classification of everything around, and for delicate aesthetic expression.

So 'the miserablest people in the world' was wholly unfounded. But it continues to reverberate, far and wide. It was in the mind of many (perhaps not all) of the first Europeans to come to live in Australia, in 1788. And it became a rationale for genocide.

5

Knowing who your relations are

The 'nuclear family' is an important grouping in what is known as western society. Basically, it consists of mother, father, sons, and daughters. One of the saddest happenings is when a family member dies. Are there terms in English to describe the people who are left behind? Just a few. We do have *widow* for a woman who has lost her husband, and *widower* for a man who has lost his wife.

Australian languages have more. In Dyirbal for instance there is *bilmbu* 'widow/widower' (these are distinguished by a gender marker; see chapter 9) and also:

mangguy	mother who has lost a child
murrgabi	father who has lost a child

For most speakers of English *orphan* is used of someone who has lost both parents (in some varieties of the language, it is applied to someone who has lost only one parent). The Ngajan dialect of Dyirbal has specific terms:

wulnggulaa	child who has lost its mother
dungun	child who has lost its father

There is in English the term *fatherless* but this is ambiguous; it can refer either to a child whose father has died, or to one born out of wedlock where the identity of the father is not known (or not revealed).

Our kinship system is centred on the nuclear family and does not extend very far beyond it. Everyone knows that the children of siblings are (first) cousins. People are also vaguely aware of the terms 'second cousin' and 'first cousin once removed'; I asked a few friends about these, and they had only a sketchy idea of their reference.

Suppose that there is a kinship arrangement:

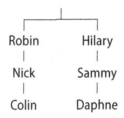

Nick and Sammy, being the children of siblings Robin and Hilary, are first cousins, typically just called cousins. Colin and Daphne, being the children of first cousins, are second cousins. Two people are in a relationship 'first cousin once removed' if one is the child of the first cousin of the other; this applies to Nick and Daphne and to Sammy and Colin.

There are a number of situations where there is no regular term in English for a certain relationship. We can mention two.

Starting from Mike (with '=' indicating the relation of marriage) we may have:

```
                        ┌──────┴──────┐
  Mike   =   Bertha       Tom      =   Sue
            wife      brother-in-law      ?
```

Tom, Mike's wife's brother, is Mike's brother-in-law. But what is the relation between Mike and Tom's wife Sue?

Now the other example:

```
  Mike              Tom
   |                 |
  John    =         Alma
  son         daughter-in-law
```

John is Mike's son and John's wife, Alma, is Mike's daughter-in-law. Alma's father, Tom, is John's father-in-law. But there is no established term in Standard English for the relationship between Mike and Tom.

Kinship terms in English are rather limited, dealing just with members of the nuclear family and a few others fairly closely related. Kinship terms in Australia are, in contrast, all-embracing. We encounter what are called 'classificatory kinship systems' in which every member of a community is in a specific relationship with every other member of the community (and, generally, of neighbouring communities too).

Basically, there about twenty or so kinship categories, and each person is in one of these with respect to each other person. From one such relationship, all others can be calculated. For instance, Bessie Jerry (Yiwaray) adopted me as her *gaya*, which is primarily 'mother's younger brother', within the Dyirbal system. I then called Bessie *daman* 'sister's child'. Bessie's daughter Marcia (Jingara) calls me *gumbu* 'mother's mother's brother' and I also call her *gumbu*. Anyone who Bessie called *yabu* '(real or classificatory) mother' would be in the *yayin* 'classificatory elder sister' category for me and I would be *yabuju* 'classificatory younger brother' to her.

Everyone is related, in some way, to everyone else. This is calculated according to a set of principles, a bit like mathematical algorithms. One principle applies all over Australia: a woman's sister counts as equivalent to that woman, and a man's brother as equivalent to that man. Other principles of calculation vary across the classificatory systems for each one of the several hundred distinct communities within Australia.

Suppose that there are around 500 people in a particular community, and around twenty kinship categories, then there would be a couple of dozen in each with respect to a particular person. For instance, in Dyirbal *yabu* is primarily 'mother' but is also used of mother's younger sisters, father's younger brothers' wives, mother's father's younger brothers' daughters, and so on.

The significant feature of such a system is that it determines who may marry who. With respect to a Dyirbal man, there will be a couple of dozen women in the category *bulgu* 'potential wife', and a spouse must be taken from this set. The details vary across the continent. For example, a Martuthunira man will marry a woman who was in the *yagan* class with respect to him; this includes mother's mother's brothers' daughters' daughters, and mother's father's sisters' daughters' daughters. The wife for a Bardi man might be mother's mother's brother's son's daughter. The class of *bulgu* 'possible wives' in Dyirbal includes father's elder sisters' child's daughters, mother's elder brothers' child's daughters, and mother's mother's younger brothers' daughters, among others.

As can be seen, the structures of Australian kinship systems are complex to the outsider. Anthropologists typically produce intricate charts which extend over several pages and are truly mind-boggling. The Dyirbal system is the one I know best (since I am integrated into it). Parts of it I shall now explain, a little at a time.

We can begin by looking at uncles and aunts and first cousins for 'ego' (the person with respect to whom the relationships are calculated) through ego's mother:

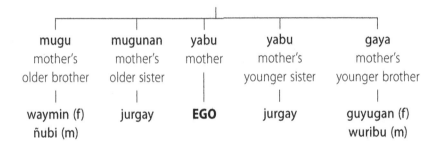

As mentioned before, a woman's sister counts as equivalent to that woman. In the diagram above, the children of mother's sisters are treated the same as mother's children; that is, as sisters and brothers of ego (*jurgay* is the general term for sibling).

There are more specific terms for older/younger brother and sister. The children of *mugunan*, mother's older sister are *mugirray* 'elder brother' and *yayin* 'elder sister' to ego, whereas the children of *yabu* 'mother's younger sister' are *yabuju* 'younger brother' and *jaman* 'younger sister' to ego. The important point here is that the older/younger designation is based on relative age at the parents' generation. In terms of actual age, a daughter of mother's elder sister, *mugunan*, may be younger than ego, but she is classed on *yayin* 'older sister' because of the age relation of her mother to ego's mother.

If anything should happen to mother, her younger sister would take care of mother's children. Indeed, the younger sister is called *yabu*, like mother. In order to distinguish them, mother's younger sister may be called *yabu jarraga*, which Dyirbal people translated into English as (real or potential) 'step-mother'.

Cousins from a same-sex link at parents' generation are called 'parallel cousins'. Indeed, trying to bring this out in English, Dyirbal people refer to them as 'cousin-sister' and 'cousin-brother'. Ego has a friendly relationship with parallel cousins, just as with actual sisters and brothers.

The term 'cross-cousins' is used where there is a different-sex link at parents' generation; that is, for the children of a mother's brother or father's sister. There is a relation of taboo between parallel cousins; a special language style has to be used in their presence (this is described in the next chapter).

The children of mother's elder brother (or father's elder sister) are:

if female: *waymin*, potential mother-in-law

if male: *ñubi*, potential father-in-law

The children of a *waymin* or *ñubi* are:

bulgu 'potential wife' if female and if ego is male

wirru 'potential husband' if male and if ego is female

ñurra if of the same sex as ego (effectively 'sister-in-law' and 'brother-in-law')

The children of mother's younger brother (or father's elder sister) are:

---

if female: *guyugan*, potential daughter-in-law

---

if male: *wuribu*, potential son-in-law

Ego's son may marry a *guyugan* and ego's daughter may marry a *wuribu*.

The chart illustrated mother's relatives. An identical scheme applies for father's relatives. His brothers' children are parallel cousins, treated by ego as brothers and sisters, and his sisters' children are cross-cousins, *waymin* and *ñubi* through an older sister, *guyugan* and *wuribu* through a younger one. Father's younger brother is named *nguma*, the same as father (or *nguma galngan* 'step-father').

In essence, one does not marry someone 'from outside'. A spouse is a relation by blood but typically not a close one. A wife will be the daughter of someone in a *waymin*, 'classificatory mother-in-law', relation to ego but is less likely to be an actual mother's older brother's daughter and more likely to be the daughter of a more distant member of the *waymin* category such as mother's father's younger sister or father's father's younger sister (according to the extended articulation of the kinship system).

Marriages were arranged, by parents (or uncles), well in advance of fruition. Typically, a girl would be promised in marriage, soon after birth, to a boy who was a few years older. The marriage could not take place until the girl reached puberty, and the boy had not only undergone the male initiation rite (which involved cicatrices being incised across the stomach) but had proved himself a good hunter and provider. Dyirbal has a verb which is apposite for use in this situation. It is *ngilbin*, whose meaning includes 'look lovingly at a promised spouse'. The girl may *ngilbin*, gaze with admiration at her promised husband as he matures into a strong and handsome youth. He, in turn, will *ngilbin*, watch lovingly as his promised wife grows to become a comely maiden, adept at assisting her mother with women's tasks.

Another verb, *gibin*, means 'provide food for relatives' and is especially used for a youth who hunts fish, wallabies, and possums for the benefit of his promised bride (*bulgu*) and her mother (*waymin*). This is done ostentatiously, so that the *waymin* will decide that the boy has proved himself and may take her daughter to his fireside.

Typically, a girl will marry a man from another local group within the same language community and go to live with him. Ida Henry (Manggañ), one of my Dyirbal teachers, said that her mother, who was from the coastal group, married a man from the tablelands group, and went to live up there. Ida was born on the tablelands then married a man from the coastal group and came down to live with him.

The differences between kinship systems is brought out by seeing how Dyirbal people deal with what the English call cousins. We can repeat the earlier diagram:

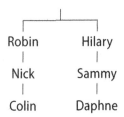

In the English system, Nick and Sammy would be called '(first) cousins' and Colin and Daphne 'second cousins', irrespective of the sex of people in the diagram, or their relative ages.

Not so in the Dyirbal system. If Robin and Hilary are of the same sex, then Nick and Sammy are parallel cousins and call each other *jurgay* 'sibling'. Now look further at what we in English call 'second cousins' (as children of parallel first cousins). If Nick and Sammy are of the same sex, then their children are again parallel cousins, who are sister/brother to each other. But if Nick and Sammy are of different sexes then their children will be cross-cousins, as shown in the diagram given above.

If Robin and Hilary are of different sexes, then Nick and Sammy are cross-cousins and the terms they use for each other vary, depending on the sex of every person in the family tree, plus the relative ages of siblings. There are even more possibilities for the 'second cousin' level through cross first cousins, but each can be worked out by applying the principles underlying this kinship system.

Even though I have only aired a portion of the Dyirbal system it does seem tricky to a person not raised within or embedded in that system. Hard to wrap one's mind around. But the original inhabitants of Australia had no difficulty in mastering this and similar systems. Their material possessions might, from a certain point of view, be denigrated as 'primitive', but their mental constructs were something else altogether. 'Miserablest?'—someone who merely strolls across a surface can have no inkling of the gold beneath.

Working out kin categories can be an absorbing pastime for the original people of Australia. Once I visited a student,

Vanessa, working on a language in Arnhem Land. So that people shouldn't get the wrong idea, she had announced in advance that I was her father's brother. As soon as I arrived we sat under a shady tree with a couple of elders as they worked out what relationship I had—through Vanessa, who had been adopted into the system—with all manner of other members of the community. It was an intellectual exercise, requiring a considerable amount of concentration.

There was mention earlier of kinship relations for which Standard English has no name. First, brother-in-law's sister, Sue, in our diagram. In Dyirbal this is straightforward:

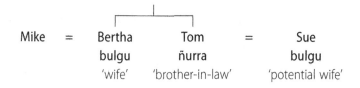

Mike's wife, Bertha, belongs to the *bulgu* category, and so does Sue, the wife of Bertha's brother Tom.

What about the other 'gap' in English kinship terminology that was pointed out: son's father-in-law, Tom, in the diagram:

```
      Mike                 Tom
        |                   |
      John      =          Alma
      galbin             guyugan
       'son'          'daughter-in-law'
```

The question could be posed: what does one call the father of a daughter-in-law? But this is putting things the wrong way round. What should be asked is: what are the classes of relative whose relationship to ego is such that ego's son may marry their daughter? There are several, including mother's younger brother and father's younger sister. Tom's relationship to Mike relates to the link between them in the kinship system (which is such that Mike's son may marry Tom's daughter), not to the fact that Alma has married John.

There are other interesting differences between systems. In English, *son* is used for a male child and *daughter* for a female one, of both mother and father. In Dyirbal *daman* is used for all children of mother (also used by her siblings) and *galbin* for all children of father (also used by his siblings). Whether a child is female or male is shown by a gender marker (explained in chapter 9).

Australian kinship systems are typically more specific than the English one. For example, each person has four grandparents. It is surely sensible to have a separate term for each, as in Dyirbal:

bulu	father's father (and his brothers and sisters)
babi	father's mother (and her sisters and brothers)
ngagi	mother's father (and his brothers and sisters)
gumbu	mother's mother (and her sisters and brothers)

English has just two terms, one for male and one for female grandparent. These are ambiguous and can lead to confusion. 'We're going to visit Grannie on Sunday,' mother announces. Little Johnny wants to know whether it is the stern grannie (mother's mother) or the generous one (father's mother). 'Do you mean

Grannie Smith or Grannie Jones?' he asks, anxiously. There is no such indeterminacy in Dyirbal; having specific labels makes for more effective communication.

One might enquire how far an Australian kinship system extends. How many generations back does it go? The answer is: as far as you want, because the system is cyclic. The key to this is that a grandparent and their grandchild address each other in the same way. For example:

gumbu, mother's mother

|

yabu, mother

|

EGO (female)

|

daman, daughter

|

gumbu, daughter's daughter (reciprocal of mother's mother)

If a grandchild calls a grandparent *gumbu* 'mother's mother' (or *bulu* or *babi* or *ngagi*) then the grandparent uses the same term to address the grandchild. That is, within the Dyirbal system, grandparent and grandchild are equivalent.

From this it follows that the parent of a grandparent is placed in the same class as the parent of a grandchild; that is, son or daughter. Similarly, the child of a grandchild is in the same class as the child of a grandparent; that is, mother or father. This can be illustrated by adding to the *gumbu* diagram:

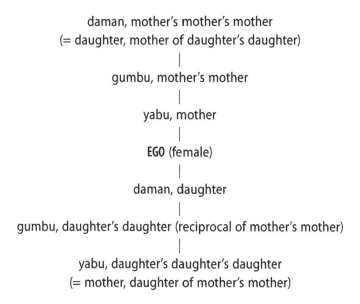

daman, mother's mother's mother
(= daughter, mother of daughter's daughter)
|
gumbu, mother's mother
|
yabu, mother
|
EGO (female)
|
daman, daughter
|
gumbu, daughter's daughter (reciprocal of mother's mother)
|
yabu, daughter's daughter's daughter
(= mother, daughter of mother's mother)

Note that while grandparent and grandchild address themselves by the same name, these differ for great-grandparent and great-grandchild. In the diagram just given they will be *daman* ('daughter') / *yabu* ('mother') to each other. (Similar diagrams apply for relatives of different sex.)

What about generations further out from ego? If there were people far enough apart in age to be great-great-grandparents and great-great-grandchildren, then the same principles would apply. Mother's mother's mother's mother would be mother's daughter, which is sister. And daughter's daughter's daughter's daughter would also be mother's daughter, also sister. That is, women four generations apart would call each other by the same term, 'sister'.

Kinship systems—right across the continent—demonstrate the mental agility of the original inhabitants of Australia. But this is not just a mind game. Each type of kin relationship carries important social obligations. One kin category may have the responsibility for organising a youth's initiation, another for performing the operation. Certain relations are involved in arranging a marriage. When a person dies, mortuary rites are to be organised by a specific relative.

Each kinship link carries expectations of how to behave. Bessie Jerry adopted me as her *gaya* 'mother's young brother' since that is an easy, friendly relationship. For the same reason our botanist friend, Tony Irvine, became Bessie's *mugirray* 'elder brother'. When we three went together into the jungle identifying plants, Bessie's friends asked 'How can you go off alone with those two white men?' Bessie explained, 'They are my *mugirray* and my *gaya*'. That made it quite proper.

At the other end of the scale, contact must be minimised between some classes of relation. For instance a *waymin* 'classificatory mother-in-law' and *wuribu* 'classificatory son-in-law' should not look at each other, let alone speak to each other directly. And when talking within earshot of such an 'avoidance' relation, a special style of language must be employed. This is the topic of the following chapter.

6

Who are you talking to?

Every language has varying styles to be used in different circumstances. For example, the words chosen, grammar employed, and—most particularly—the intonation used will be quite different between a political oration and an amorous soliloquy. Poetry differs from official letter-writing in toying with unusual words and structures.

In many languages of East Asia there are markedly different speech styles. If someone in Thailand is speaking to, or in the presence of, a member of the royal family, a special vocabulary must be used, called 'Royal Thai'. Before a sentence can be planned in Korean, the speaker must take into account their relationship to the addressee in terms of age, social status, kinship, in-group membership, and also the context of utterance. There are in Korean half a dozen distinct speech styles characterised by—among other features—emblematic endings on verbs.

Each of the original languages of Australia had a special song style. This typically differed from the everyday language style in accentuation and in grammatical possibilities. There was often a special set of words used only in songs (a number of these might have archaic form). Some—but by no means all—Australian communities had a special speech style which was taught to youths at initiation, and used only among initiated men (being hidden from women and children). (Initiation registers and song styles were illustrated at the end of chapter 3.)

In every Australian community there were certain classes of kin with whom contact should be avoided, or kept to a minimum. Typically, a mother-in-law and son-in-law should not look at one another, nor sit or stand close together. In many (perhaps in all) groups there was some linguistic marker of an avoidance relationship. This sometimes consisted of a score or so special words which had to be used in place of everyday terms (perhaps for 'animal', 'person', 'fire', 'water', and a handful more). Some languages had one or two hundred words in the 'avoidance vocabulary'; other words would be the same as in the everyday style. For just a couple of languages, every lexical word (that is, every noun, verb, and adjective in the vocabulary) was different.

In Bunuba, spoken around the Fitzroy River in north Western Australia, the avoidance style—called Gun.gunma—was used by a man when within earshot of a real or classificatory mother-in-law, and she would use it back. Gun.gunma consisted of about two hundred special lexical words and a few distinctive grammatical features such as extended use of an auxiliary verb.

We encounter a similar situation on the other side of the continent, for Guugu Yimidhiir, the nation James Cook met in 1770. Here one could not say anything when a real or classificatory mother-in-law was within hearing. But in the presence of a brother-in-law, father-in-law, and certain other relatives, a man had to look away from him and speak in a slow, soft and respectful tone of voice, and to substitute avoidance equivalents for many common words.

The table illustrates the difference between the two styles in the two languages, for four lexical words:

BUNUBA			GUUGU YIMIDHIRR	
everyday style	*avoidance style*		*everyday style*	*avoidance style*
garuwa	ngawagi	'water'	buurraay	wabirr
tharra	jurrumbulu	'tame dog'	gudaa	guguur
jamayina	mayirnday	'axe'	warrbi	gadiilbaga
thinga	jarrgambirri	'foot'	dhamal	buyiibuyii

In Dyirbal, 300 kilometres to the south of Guugu Yimidhirr, the everyday speech style was called Guwal and the avoidance style Jalnguy (referred to in English as 'mother-in-law language'). Every single lexeme was different between Guwal and Jalnguy: every noun, every verb, every adjective, and every time word. In contrast, the grammar was the same.

As an illustration, look at how one would say, 'I gave that bush guava fruit to mother', first in the everyday style, Guwal, and then in Jalnguy, which must be used when within hearing of an 'avoidance relation', such as mother-in-law:

GUWAL	Ngaja	[bala-m	muja]	wuga-n	yabu-gu
	I	THAT-EDIBLE	bush.guava	give-PAST	mother-TO
JALNGUY	Ngaja	[bala-m	gumalam]	jayma-n	ngarmbu-gu

I gave that bush guava fruit to mother

Grammatical items stay the same: affixes such as 'past tense' -*n* on a verb, and ending -*gu* 'to, for' on a noun, together with grammatical words such as the pronoun *ngaja* 'I' and the noun marker *balam*. The first part of this, *bala*-, states that the fruit of the bush guava is '(visible and) there' and the final -*m* indicates that it goes under gender III, which covers all edible plants. (The gender system is discussed in chapter 9.)

But lexical words are all different. Guwal verb *wuga*- 'give' is rendered by *jayma*- in Jalnguy, and nouns *yabu* 'mother' and *muja* 'bush guava' by *ngarmbu* and *gumalam* respectively.

The reader may exclaim: does a speaker of Dyirbal have to learn two whole vocabularies, one in Guwal and one in Jalnguy? Well yes, but it is not twice as many words. In many instances, a single word in Jalnguy will correspond to a whole group of words in Guwal.

In Guwal, every plant and animal has a specific designation. Consider names for possums, for instance. These include:

midin, 'common ringtail possum, *Pseudocheirus peregrinus*'

jula, 'green ringtail possum, *Pseudocheirus archeri*'

mungañ, 'Herbert River ringtail possum, *Pseudochirulus herbertiensis*'

yabi, 'common brushtail possum, *Trichosurus johnstonii*'

In Jalnguy the name *jibuñ* is used for all of these, plus three other types of possum, three sugar gliders, and a flying squirrel.

The principle is straightforward. When speaking Guwal one must be as specific as possible, never vague. Being vague is considered a mark of foolishness, or of lack of brain. If a snake is remarked on, it must if at all possible be identified. (This is sensible for survival, since several of the most deadly snakes in the world slither around in Dyirbal country amid the rainforest south of Cairns.) Guwal does have a generic term *wadam* 'snake' but this would only be used if, for instance, you noticed the tail of a snake disappearing into the undergrowth but could not see enough for an identification. Guwal has no generic term 'possum' since here species identification should always be possible.

Contrasted with the requirement for precise identification when speaking Guwal, the Jalnguy style operates with generic terms. This accords with the social context in which it is used—it is appropriate to be vague in a kin-avoidance situation. Of course, a Jalnguy description can be made more specific if needed; for instance, by adding a relative clause to *jibuñ* 'possum, sugar glider, or flying squirrel', describing colouring, habitat, or some other distinctive feature. But this would seldom be resorted to.

In the past, people attempting to disparage the original languages of Australia maintained that they have no generic terms, indicating that their speakers cannot think in the abstract. I have also heard the opposite opinion, that they only have words with a broad meaning, nothing precise. Dyirbal serves to refute both false impressions: in everyday speech one must be specific, but when discoursing in a context requiring extreme respect, it is appropriate to express things on a more general level.

Some important terms have a one-to-one correspondence between Guwal and Jalnguy. For instance, *ngarmbu* in Jalnguy corresponds just to *yabu* 'mother, mother's younger sister, etc.,' in Guwal. There are also one-to-one correspondences for some of the staple foodstuffs. For example:

GUWAL	JALNGUY		
mirrañ	dirraba	'black bean'	(*Castanospermum australe*)
jubula	manji	'black pine'	(*Prumnopitys amarus*)
guway	gadaginay	'brown walnut'	(*Endiandra palmerstonii*)

(The lengthy preparation needed to make black beans edible was described near the beginning of chapter 3.)

There is often a single term in Jalnguy for a whole set of plants which have a common feature. In the sentence quoted a couple of pages back, *gumalam* was given as Jalnguy for the Guwal noun *muja* 'bush guava (*Eupomatia laurina*)', a fruit which can be eaten raw. In fact the term *gumalam* covers about twenty fruits which may be eaten raw (all with individual names in Guwal): figs, cherries, wild raspberry, native apples, gingers, wild banana, and also recent introductions such as mango, orange, and mandarin.

Six types of lawyer vine (all species within the genus *Calamus*) have distinct names in Guwal but are grouped together as *ngunjanum* in Jalnguy. Blankets were made from the bark of five fig trees with separate Guwal names: *balun* (*Ficus obliqua*), *banba* (*Ficus destruens*), *gibar* (*Ficus virens*), *magurra* (*Ficus variegata*), and *wirra* (*Ficus opposita*). In Jalnguy these are all *muyñarri*, which is also the Jalnguy term for 'traditional blanket' (*gambila* in Guwal).

A similar principle applies for names of body parts. Jalnguy noun *winarra* is the correspondent for five Guwal terms: *jina* 'foot (of a person)', *nguru* 'heel', *gadam* 'sole of the foot', *murun* 'paw of a dog', and *magal* 'back paw of a kangaroo or wallaby'. However, some important body parts do have a unique correspondent; for example, Jalnguy *ngun.ngun* corresponds just to Guwal *ngamun* 'breast'.

The previous chapter outlined the classificatory kinship systems of the original people of Australia. Each person is placed in one of about twenty kin classes with respect to ego. Some relationships are marked by jovial interchange, some by a fair degree of familiarity, and others by avoidance. In the Dyirbal system, the categories of *waymin*, *ñubi*, *guyugan*, and *wuribu*—potential mother-in-law, father-in-law, daughter-in-law, and son-in-law—demanded mutual avoidance.

A speaker of Dyirbal should not look directly at an avoidance relation, and should not speak directly to them. Instead, communication would be through a third party. Sitting as far as possible from his *waymin*, a man could say to his wife, in Jalnguy: 'Would your mother like some more meat, from the wallaby which I just killed?' The *waymin* would respond through the same channel. The avoidance relationship was always reciprocal: if X used Jalnguy in the presence of Y, then Y should use it in the presence of X.

Unlike in Guugu Yimidhirr, Jalnguy appears to have been spoken in the same tone of voice as Guwal, the entirely separate vocabulary being sufficient to mark it as a respect register. I was told that Jalnguy was learnt in a natural way, like Guwal but a few years behind it. In terms of the classificatory kinship system, each person would have, from birth, a full set of avoidance relations, potential 'in-laws'. A boy would hear Jalnguy spoken around him and would be encouraged to use it himself—by the age of eight or so—in the presence of any woman who was in *waymin* relationship to him. By the onset of puberty, it would be obligatory to do so.

In some Australian communities there is a separate speech style which is used at male initiation. For speakers of Dyirbal, this was a secondary function of Jalnguy. The initiation ceremony involved the incision of two or three cicatrices across the belly. As soon as the cuts were made, some older men would go out in search of eels, leaving the newly initiated youths with a number of guardians. For two or three days the initiands were not permitted to speak. Then the elders would return with eels, give the flesh to the youths to eat, and anoint the wounds with grease from pieces of chewed eel. During the two- or three-day-long eel ceremony, the initiands could talk to the older men, but only in Jalnguy (note that these were not avoidance kin); they would be answered in Guwal. It appears that this was the only circumstance in which the use of Jalnguy was not reciprocal.

Let's look a little further at the many-to-one correspondences between Guwal and Jalnguy vocabularies. Terms for relative time include:

	GUWAL	JALNGUY
'tomorrow'	ngulga	ganba-gabun
'later on today'	gilu	ganba
'earlier on today'	jañjarru	ganba
'yesterday'	ngumbungga	ganba-gabun
'a few days ago'	ngudangga	ganba-gabun

In Jalnguy, each word indicates a certain distance from now: *ganba* 'within today' and *ganba-gabun* 'outside of today' (note that *-gabun* is a regular grammatical suffix 'another'). There is no distinction in the Jalnguy terms between future time and past time. How can this work? Quite naturally, by the tense inflection on the verb. If *ganba* is used with a verb in past tense it indicates 'earlier on today' and with a verb in future tense it is 'later on today'. Guwal indicates time twice, in lexical words and in grammar; Jalnguy simply shows it once.

In essence, the avoidance style is organised in such a way that it is possible to say in Jalnguy anything which can be said in Guwal, but at a more general level (although a statement in Jalnguy can be made more specific, if this should be required).

As European-type society encroached on speakers of Dyirbal, traditional practices gradually diminished. The last male initiation was held in the 1920s. People said that Jalnguy stopped being used around 1930. When I began to learn and analyse the language, in the 1960s, there were quite a few elderly people who had used Jalnguy when they were young and were glad to discuss it with me. I recorded several conversations in Jalnguy and went through a couple of thousand Guwal words, asking for the Jalnguy correspondent of each.

The way a single Jalnguy verb was given for several Guwal verbs proved to be particularly interesting. For example, my notebook reads (quoting verbs in past/present form):

GUWAL VERB		JALNGUY CORRESPONDENT
wugan	'give'	jayman
gibin	'provide (food) for relatives especially promised wife and her mother and family'	jayman
gulnggan	'breastfeed'	jayman

As the next stage of investigation, I took a Jalnguy verb and asked which Guwal verbs corresponded to it. 'How about *jayman*?', I asked Chloe Grant. 'That would be *wugan*', she replied. This is plainly the central verb of 'giving'. 'How about *gibin* and *gulnggan*?', I persisted. 'Yes,' Chloe agreed, 'they'd be *jayman* too.'

'In Guwal there's a difference between *wugan* and *gibin*?', I enquired. 'Oh yes,' Chloe agreed. 'How would you bring that out in Jalnguy then?' Chloe thought for a moment or two. 'Well, *wugan* would be just plain *jayman*, and for *gibin* you'd say *jayma-jayman*.' Any verb in Dyirbal may have its first two syllables repeated (this is called 'reduplication') with the meaning 'do a lot, do to excess'. *Miyandañu* means 'laugh' and *miya-miyandañu* is 'laugh a lot'. Using reduplicated *jayma-jayman* as Jalnguy for *gibin* conveys the sense of this Guwal verb—giving in a rather ostentatious manner, so as to suggest that the boy who does the giving has proved himself as a competent hunter and should be allowed to claim his promised wife. (This is mentioned in the previous chapter.)

Chloe then thought about the difference between *wugan* and *gulnggan*, 'For *wugan* you'd just say *jayman*, and *gulnggan* would be *ngun.ngun-du jayman* in Jalnguy'. *Ngun.ngun* is the Jalnguy for 'breast' (*ngamun* in Guwal) and suffix *-du* means 'with': 'give with the breast', a perfect correspondent in Jalnguy for the Guwal verb *gulnggan*.

Similar results were obtained with other verbs. For instance, *jurrmbayban* was given as the Jalnguy correspondent for several Guwal verbs, including *jurran* 'rub', *ñamban* 'plaster, paint with the flat of the hand', and *banggan* 'draw or paint with the finger,' nowadays extended to 'write'. When Guwal equivalents were sought for the Jalnguy verb *jurrmbayban*, Chloe gave just *jurran*. For *ñamban* 'hand-with' was added and for *banggan* 'finger-with' was added.

Isn't Jalnguy an ingenious and insightful system? What we have is the underlying semantic system being realised at two levels: one general and one specific. This naturally shows how speakers of Dyirbal classify animals and plants, and the way related kinds of activity are linked together.

We have been examining aspects of language structure. But a language does not exist just on paper. It is primarily spoken and to properly appreciate the original languages of Australia it is important to learn how to speak them.

7

Getting your tongue around it

Suppose that you want to achieve a more-or-less correct pronunciation for words in one of the original languages of Australia. This is not difficult but, as for the learner of any language containing unfamiliar or 'unusual' sounds, it does require a little application.

Let's commence with a cautionary tale. A young teacher, just out of college, was sent to a school in the bush where most of the children were familiar with the local language, as well as with English. The teacher's course had included nothing whatsoever about the culture, ethnicity, or languages of the original peoples of Australia.

The teacher was keen to connect with his pupils. Desks were in four columns and he had the idea of giving each a name in the local language. The pupils joined in enthusiastically. He suggested that the first column be named 'possum'. How do you say that: *yawa*. The teacher repeated this, to nods of approval. Next column 'python', *gabul*, third one 'frog', *yuday*. All was going well. Then he came to the last column of desks. What about 'turtle'? Fine. The name was supplied—*ngujay*. This begins with a sound that occurs at the end of a word in English, as in *bang*, or in the middle, as in *singer*. The 'ng' sound never comes at the beginning of a word in English and speakers of English—unless they have had a little training—have difficulty in pronouncing it word-initially.

The schoolteacher couldn't do it. *'Ngujay'*, all the pupils were shouting. He tried to say it: *'nujay'*. 'No, no, sir, it's *ngujay'*. Another attempt: *'mujay'*. The class collapsed into laughter. Good intentions thwarted, that teacher never again tried to pronounce any word in the local language.

Although conventionally written with two letters, as 'ng', there is just a single sound before the first vowel in the schoolmaster's word 'turtle', and after the vowel in English words like *bang* and *sing*. The phonetic symbol for this sound is /ŋ/. It will make things clearer if we write it as /ŋ/ for the next few pages. (It is given as 'ng' in the remainder of the book.)

Being able to say /ŋ/ at the beginning of a word is probably the most important skill to master if you want to pronounce words in an Australian language. And it really is quite easy. Suppose that you want to say the word for 'yes' in Dyirbal, which is /ŋa/. There are several ways of going about this.

- Say the English word *bang* which is /baŋ/. Add an /a/ at the end, giving /baŋa/. (Make sure you don't put a /g/ in there: say /baŋa/ and not /baŋga/.) Repeat the word a few times and then drop off the initial /ba/. Thus /baŋa/, /baŋa/, /ŋa/, /ŋa/. There, you've got it!

- Another technique is to put your tongue in position to say /g/ and then, without moving the tongue, try to say /n/. It will come out as /ŋ/.

No two languages have exactly the same set of sounds. For example, French has nasalised vowels (that is vowels pronounced through the nose), which English lacks, and English has sounds written as 'th'—as in *this* and *thin*—which French lacks.

Each language has a set of what are called 'phonemes' (which make up the 'phonological system'). If you substitute one phoneme for another in a word it changes the meaning. For example, /b/ and /p/ are distinct phonemes in English. Take the word *bin*. If you substitute *p* for the *b*, you get *pin*, which has a different meaning from *bin*. This shows that in this language /b/ and /p/ are separate phonemes.

The ideal alphabet has a single letter for each phoneme. Spanish is almost like this. Alphabets devised for Australian languages are all pretty good. The English alphabet is far from ideal, which is why it is not a good idea to try to write words from Australian languages as if they were some sort of ersatz English.

A phoneme is likely to have a number of variant pronunciations, depending on various factors, including which dialect of the language is being used. A good example is the *r* sound in English. For most speakers in Australia and England it has a smooth pronunciation whereas in Scotland it is typically a rolled sound. However, these are not separate phonemes, but merely alternative ways of saying the same phoneme. A speaker from Adelaide will say *arrow* with a smooth *r*-sound and someone from Glasgow may accord it a healthy roll. But it is the same word; changing the pronunciation of the /r/ doesn't alter the meaning. That is, there is just one /r/ phoneme in English, which can be pronounced in several ways.

Australian languages differ. There are generally two *r* phonemes: one with a smooth pronunciation, very much like the *r* -sound in

Australian English (but with the tongue tip turned a little further back in the mouth). And one with a rolled pronunciation, similar to Scottish English. It is convenient to write the smooth one as *r* and the rolled one as *rr*.

This can be illustrated with a pair of words from Dyirbal:

buru	'elbow'
burru	'rhinoceros beetle (and its grub)'

If you substitute one *r* sound for the other, this produces a different word, showing that *r* and *rr* are distinct phonemes in Dyirbal.

We have seen that what are alternative pronunciations of a single phoneme in English are contrasting phonemes in this— as in other—Australian languages. And the same thing happens the other way round. In English the voiced bilabial stop /b/ is a different phoneme from the voiceless bilabial stop /p/. But in most Australian languages the two sounds are variant pronunciations of a single phoneme. For example, you can say either *buru* or *puru* and it is the same word, 'elbow'; similarly for *burru* and *purru*. Substituting *p* for *b* in Dyirbal does not affect the meaning; it is the same word, just pronounced in a slightly different way.

We see that while English has two bilabial stop phonemes, voiced /b/ and voiceless /p/, Dyirbal and many other Australian languages have just one bilabial stop phoneme, with variant pronunciation, either voiced or voiceless. How should it be written? Well, there are two alternatives in the Roman alphabet (used for English and very many other languages) and either may be used. The single bilabial stop in Dyirbal can be written as either *b* or *p*. The only requirement is consistency: choose one letter and stick to it.

Similar pairs of stops in English also correspond to a single phoneme in most Australian languages. Alongside /b/ and /p/, these include /d/ and /t/, and /g/ and /k/. The convention is either to use *b*, *d*, and *g*, or else *p*, *t*, and *k* (and not to muddle them up). In a language where these phonemes are mostly pronounced voiced, *b*, *d*, and *g* may be preferred; where they are mostly pronounced unvoiced, then *p*, *t*, and *k* may be considered most appropriate.

Dyirbal has quite a small number of consonant phonemes, just thirteen. As we shall see shortly, some languages have more, but they always include these thirteen. There are *w* and *y*, very much as in English, plus *r* and *rr*, which have already been mentioned. And nine more, set out in the box. (An interesting feature is that nearly all Australian languages lack the sounds that linguists call 'fricatives' and 'sibilants': there is no *f*, *v*, *h*, *s*, *z*, etc.)

place of articulation	stop	nasal	lateral
bottom lip against top lip (bilabial)	b	m	
tongue tip against ridge behind upper front teeth (apico-alveolar)	d	n	l
blade of tongue against hard palate (lamino-palatal)	j	ñ	
back of tongue against velum or soft palate (doreo-velar)	g	ŋ	

Seven of the phonemes in the box are pronounced very much as in English. Just the lamino-palatals are a little different. It is convenient to write the lamino-palatal stop as *j* (alternatives are *dj* or *dy*). It can be approximated by English *j*, as in *jelly* and *major*. But it is in fact a sharper sound, a stop similar to *b*, *d*, and *g*—like pronouncing *d* and *y* simultaneously. The lamino-palatal nasal can be written *ñ*, like the sound in Spanish (alternatives are *nj* or *ny*). The nearest thing in English is the nasal in the middle of *onion*, like an *n* and a *y* said simultaneously.

Many languages have more than these four series of stops and nasals. For instance, Guugu Yimidhirr also has:

place of articulation	stop	nasal
blade of tongue against teeth (lamino-dental)	dh	nh

If one of *j*, *dh*, or *d* is substituted for another a new word results, confirming that these are distinct phonemes. For example:

maji	'rain'
madhi	'embraced'
madimadi	'maggot'

Another addition to the four basic series of stops and nasals are the following phonemes, found in Bardi:

place of articulation	stop	nasal	lateral
tongue tip turned back so that its underside touches the hard palate (retroflex)	rd	rn	rl

Retroflex phonemes are found in many of the languages of India. Speakers of Indian languages typically accord a retroflex pronunciation to English /d/ and /t/ (but here they are not separate phonemes, just alternative ways of saying /d/ and /t/).

Quite a few languages have six series of stops and nasals, including both lamino-dental and retroflex. Bunuba is of this type, with contrasting /b/, /d/, /rd/, /dh/, /j/, and /g/, and a similar set of nasals. (A particular feature of Australian languages is that there is almost always a nasal corresponding to each stop phoneme.)

Languages in the eastern part of the continent—including Guugu Yimidhirr and Dyirbal—have a single lateral phoneme, apico-alveolar /l/, just like English. Elsewhere there are more, sometimes one in each of the apical and laminal series. Thus Bardi has three: apico-alveolar /l/, retroflex /rl/, and lamino-palatal /ly/. To these Arrernte (or Aranda), spoken around Alice Springs, adds lamino-dental /lh/.

A typical Australian language has two kinds of syllable: CV and CVC (where C is a consonant and V a vowel). Many languages have no monosyllables, or else very few (for instance, Dyirbal just has interjections *ŋa* 'yes' and *ŋu* 'alright'). Most words thus consist of two or more syllables.

The possibilities for a word of two syllables are:

CVCV, CVCVC, CVCCV, CVCCVC

The basic features are:

- A word always begins with a single consonant, not with two consonants nor with a vowel.
- It may end in either a consonant or a vowel.
- Between each two vowels there will be either a single consonant or a sequence of two consonants.
- There is never a sequence of vowels.

Some consonant phonemes are generally written as a sequence of two letters, making it straightforward to type up the language on a standard keyboard. There is no /h/ phoneme so that the lamino-dentals can be written as *dh*, *nh*, and *lh* without the possibility of confusion. Generally, phoneme /r/ cannot be followed by /d/, /n/, or /l/, so that writing the retroflexes as *rd*, *rn*, and *rl* also does not lead to confusion.

However, things are a bit trickier for the dorso-velar nasal /ŋ/. It is sensible to write it as *ng* (as in English) but it is then necessary to distinguish between the single sound /ŋ/ and a sequence of /n/ plus /g/. Ambiguity can be avoided by placing a full stop between *n* and *g*. Illustrating from Dyirbal, we have:

/buŋgu/	'knee'	*written as*	bunggu
/bungu/	'maggot'	*written as*	bun.gu
/buṇalu/	'tabooed'	*written as*	bungalu

The name for 'tame dog' in Dharuk, the language from around Sydney, is written as *din.gu* (to show that it is /dingu/ and not /diŋgu/ or /diṇu/). The avoidance style in Bunuba is written Gun.gunma.

We can now look at vowels. Latin had five vowel phonemes and there was a letter for each in its alphabet—the familiar *a, e, i, o, u*. English uses the Latin alphabet, but it has seven short and five long vowels plus eight diphthongs. There aren't enough vowel letters to express the vowel phonemes in a systematic way, so all sorts of tricks are used. For example, *bit* is a monosyllabic word with vowel /i/. Add a final -*e* to the written form of the word and we get *bite*, still a monosyllable but with diphthong /ai/.

There are several quite different ways of writing one phoneme in modern English orthography. For instance, /u/ is represented by letter *u* in *full* and *put*, by *o* in *wolf*, by *oo* in *good*, and by *ou* in *could*; it is the same vowel phoneme in each word.

Orthographies for Australian languages are systematic, consistently employing one letter for each vowel phoneme. It is easy to do this, using the Latin alphabet, since most Australian languages have fewer vowels than English (or Latin). In fact, about two-thirds of them have just three vowel phonemes, as set out in the box.

	like the sound in Standard English	
i	front of the tongue is raised towards the hard palate	pit
u	back of the tongue is raised towards the soft palate or velum	put
a	tongue is kept low in the mouth	pat

Each vowel can have a range of pronunciations. Take the word for 'stone' in Dyirbal, /diban/. The first vowel is normally pronounced like that in Standard English *pit*. However, the tongue is sometimes a little lower in the front of the mouth, like that in English *pet*. Whether pronounced as [diban] or [deban] it is recognised as the same word, 'stone'. Thus, while /i/ and /e/ are contrasting phonemes for English, in Dyirbal—as in most other Australian languages— [i] and [e] are variant pronunciations of one phoneme. This is invariably written as *i*, rather than as *e*, since the most common pronunciation is as [i].

Some languages just have three short vowels. In others, each vowel exists in both short and long forms. For long vowels the articulation is lengthened, this being appropriately shown in writing by doubling the vowel letter. There are thus six vowel phonemes: /i/, /u/, /a/, and /ii/, /uu/, /aa/. For instance, in Warrgamay (spoken on the lower Herbert River, immediately to the south of Dyirbal), the phonemic status of short and long vowels is demonstrated by:

badi-	'to hook a fish'	baadi-	'to cry, weep'
giba	'liver'	giiba-	'to scratch'
jurra	'cloud, sky'	juurra-	'to rub'

Some languages have larger systems of vowels, with four, five, or even more members (leaving aside length). Sometimes it is possible to see how the additional vowels developed historically. For example:

/a/ followed by /y/ became /e/

/a/ followed by /w/ became /o/

Most words in English have primary stress on just one syllable, which has a full vowel. Unstressed syllables are typically reduced to be a short vowel pronounced in the middle of the mouth, called 'schwa', written /ə/. For example (with stress shown by an acute accent on that vowel):

woman /wúmən/	*talcum* /tálkəm/	*ribbon* /ríbən/

In these words, vowels written as *a*, *u*, and *o* are all pronounced as a schwa, /ə/. Going the other way round, the schwa sound may be represented by a variety of letters.

Most typically, a word in an Australian language is stressed (or accented) on the first syllable. But, unlike in English, the vowels in unstressed syllables are always clearly pronounced, never reduced. For instance, the word for 'black pine' (*Prumnopitys amarus*) in Dyirbal is *júbula*. Its pronunciation can be indicated by *jóó-boo-la*.

A principle which must be observed when attempting to pronounce a word in one of the original languages of Australia is: **always pronounce each vowel clearly, never reduce them to a schwa, as happens in English.**

Frequently, well-intentioned speakers try to articulate words as they would in English. This can lead to unrecognisable pronunciations, giving rise to erroneous spellings. For instance:

traditional pronunciation	/júbula/
anglicised pronunciation	/júbələ/

As was just shown, the central vowel /ə/ in English is represented in the orthography in many ways, including by *a*, *o*, or *u*. Someone pronouncing the word for 'black pine' as /jubələ/ may now write it as *jubolo* or *jubalu* or in one of many other ways. The anglicised pronunciation and consequent re-spelling could render the word unrecognisable to someone fluent in the traditional language.

When working out the most suitable orthography for a language, decisions have to be made. Insights from grammar may assist in choosing between alternative analyses. This can be illustrated from Dyirbal.

Whereas English uses prepositions—such as *on*, *in*, *at*—to specify kinds of location, Australian languages employ a locative case suffix (indicating 'at' or 'in' or 'on') to a noun. The locative suffix in Dyirbal has various forms, depending on the final phoneme of the word it is added to:

- After a word ending in a vowel, the locative case is *-ŋga*. For example:

gandi	'ledge'	gandi-ŋga	'on a ledge'
mila	'clearing'	mila-ŋga	'in a clearing'
wabu	'thick jungle'	wabu-ŋga	'in the thick jungle'

- After a word ending in a nasal, the locative case consists of a stop with the same place of articulation as the nasal, plus *a*. That is, *-ba* after *m*, *-da* after *n*, and *-ja* after *ñ* (no word in Dyirbal ends in *ŋ*). For example:

mujam	'wart'	mujam-ba	'on a wart'
muṇan	'mountain'	muṇan-da	'on a mountain'
birriñ	'sea'	birriñ-ja	'in the sea'

Now the problem to be solved. The word for 'road' is pronounced [yalgai], rhyming with *my* /mai/ in English. There are two alternatives:

| write it as *yalgai*, ending in a vowel |
| write it as *yalgay*, ending in a consonant |

Which of these is most appropriate? One can tell by checking the form of the locative case suffix for this word. If it ended in a vowel, we would expect *-ŋga*. But in fact locative case is *-ja*, a stop with the same place of articulation (lamino-palatal) as the semi-vowel *y*. That is:

---

yalgay   'road'   yalgay-ja   'on a road'

This fits in with the overall analysis of the language. As mentioned before, Dyirbal—like almost all other Australian languages—allows a word to include two consonants together, but never two vowels together.

In the past, people have found many ways to disparage the original languages of Australia. 'They have no grammar.' 'Only a couple of hundred words.' 'No generic terms.' And the most damning of all: 'They don't have a proper language, just a collection of grunts and groans.'

This chapter has provided a glimpse into the sophisticated phonological systems—phonemes, syllable and word structures, and so on—of the languages. All the components of the overall system of a language knit together, as was just demonstrated through grammatical criteria deciding that /yalgay/ is the appropriate phonemic representation of the word for 'road' in Dyirbal.

We can now investigate grammar. How a word is built up from smaller bits of meaning, and how words are fitted together to construct sentences.

8

Putting the bits together

Australian languages—like all others—have ways of marking statements, commands and questions, of showing negation, of marking possession, and so on.

Across the languages of the world, there is always some means for indicating the time when an activity took place, most often by adding tense affixes to a verb. English has a rather rudimentary tense system, with just two members, illustrated by:

PRESENT	The meat smell-s bad
PAST	The meat smell-ed (*or* smel-t) bad

In English, future time is shown not by a tense suffix to the verb but by what linguists call a preposed modal: *will*, *shall*, or *be going to*.

Many Australian languages have a fuller tense system. The most extensive one is found in the language spoken on the western islands of Torres Strait, between the Australian mainland and New Guinea (these islands are part of Australia). West Torres shows some similarities with languages spoken across the continent, but also a number of differences. For example: there are six vowels, and sibilants /s/ and /z/; also, words may commence with a vowel.

West Torres has at least four past tenses. These can be illustrated by sample sentences with pronoun *ngay* 'I', verb *uzar-* 'go', and suffix *-ka* 'to' added to the place name *Pulu*:

Ngay uzar-aydhin Pulu-ka	I went to Pulu some time before yesterday
Ngay uzar-ayngul Pulu-ka	I went to Pulu yesterday
Ngay uzar-ibungel Pulu-ka	I went to Pulu last night
Ngay uzar-ima Pulu-ka	I went to Pulu earlier today

Suffix *-i* is used for an activity just completed (it could be regarded as a fifth type of past tense) or for something taking place now:

Ngay uzar-i Pulu-ka	I just went to Pulu *or* I am going to Pulu now

And there are three future tenses:

Ngay uzar-ika Pulu-ka	I will go to Pulu later on today
Ngay uzar-ekay Pulu-ka	I will go to Pulu tomorrow
Ngay uzar-aykakay Pulu-ka	I will go to Pulu some time after tomorrow

These tense suffixes apply when the subject is singular, referring to just one person. There are different suffixes when the subject is dual (referring to two people) or plural (referring to more than two). There are also quite a few irregular verbs just as there are in English where the past tenses of *sing* and *go* are *sang* and *went* (rather than the regular forms *sing-ed* and *go-ed*), but on a much greater scale.

The original languages of Australia have far more complex verb structures than English. There can be affixes indicating 'do quickly', 'do repeatedly or continuously', 'do a bit', 'do of necessity' and 'do in the morning', among many others.

There are many instances where what would have to be shown by a separate word in English is rendered by a grammatical affix in an Australian language. A noun in Dyirbal may take suffix *-gabun* 'another' or *-jarran* 'two, a pair' (and there are a dozen others). Thus: *yara-gabun* 'another man', and *yara-jarran* 'two men, a pair of men'. Suffixes can be combined, in either order and with a difference of meaning:

yara-gabun-jarran	'two more men'
yara-jarran-gabun	'another pair of men' (this would be appropriate if the men were arranged in pairs)

Intricate systems of pronouns are a speciality of Australian languages. In Standard English we have singular and plural first person pronouns—*I/me* and *we/us*—but only one form for second person form, *you*, covering both singular and plural (and used for object as well as subject function).

In contrast, Australian languages invariably have separate pronouns for singular, dual (referring to two people), and plural (indicating more than two people), sometimes distinct forms for singular, dual, trial (referring to three people), and plural (here indicating more than three).

Another useful feature is to distinguish two forms of *us*—whether it includes you ('me and you') or excludes you ('me and people other than you'). For example, there are two first person dual pronouns in Guugu Yimidhirr (spoken around Cooktown):

1st dual inclusive	ngali	'me and you'
1st dual exclusive	ngaliinh	'me and someone else, not you'

Compare this with what happens in English. Suppose that Tom says to his assistant Jake 'We've been invited to the boss's for dinner'. On hearing this, Jake doesn't know whether 'we' refers to Tom and his wife (an exclusive meaning) or to Tom and Jake (an inclusive one). If they had been talking Guugu Yimidhirr, things would have been totally clear. Jake would then know whether to respond 'I hope you two enjoy it' (if the exclusive pronoun had been used) or 'Great, I'll look forward to it' (for the inclusive pronoun).

As described in chapter 5, kinship links loom large for the original inhabitants of Australia. And they permeate the grammar. An engaging example of this comes from Lardil, spoken on Mornington Island in the Gulf of Carpentaria. Here there are two sets of pronouns; which one is used depends on whether the people referred to are in a 'harmonic' or a 'disharmonic' relationship.

HARMONIC RELATIONSHIP: in the same generation or two generations apart, for example, brothers and sisters, ego and grandparent or grandchild.

DISHARMONIC RELATIONSHIP: one or three generations apart, for example, ego and parent, uncle or aunt, or son or daughter; ego and great-grandparent or great-grandchild.

The dual pronouns (referring to two people) are:

	HARMONIC	DISHARMONIC
1st person inclusive 'you and I'	ngaku-rri	ngaku-ni
1st person exclusive 'he/she and I'	ña-rri	ña-anki
2nd person 'you two'	ki-rri	ñi-inki
3rd person 'them two'	pi-rri	rni-inki

Suppose that you want to ask 'Where will you two go?' If the two people addressed belong to the same generation or are two generations apart, you would use the harmonic 2nd person dual pronoun:

Karan-kur	waang-kur	ki-rri?
WHERE-FUTURE	go-FUTURE	2du:HARMONIC

And if the people addressed are one or three generations apart then the corresponding disharmonic pronoun would be used:

Karan-kur	waang-kur	ñi-inki?
WHERE-FUTURE	go-FUTURE	2du:DISHARMONIC

In many Australian languages pronouns are separate words, as they are in English. This is shown in the Lardil sentences just quoted and in those from West Torres at the very beginning of this chapter. But in slightly more than half the languages things are rather more complex. What we then get is pronouns being affixes to the verb; these are called 'bound pronouns'. A verb thus contains information about its subject and can make up a complete sentence all on its own.

This can be exemplified from Nyigina, spoken in northern Western Australia just inland from Bardi. (Bardi and Nyigina are distinct languages, but closely genetically related, in a similar way to French and Italian):

Ngan-a-ibi

I(SUBJECT)-FUTURE-drink

I will drink

The subject prefix would be *wal-* for 'you (singular)', *yan-* for 'you and me', *wan-* for 'he/she', and so on. Pronouns also exist as separate words (called 'free pronouns'), but these are as a rule used sparingly and for contrast, in order to emphasise that the subject *is* this person and not another. For example, *ngayu* ('I') *ngan-a-ibi* 'I (not someone else) will drink'.

If the verb requires an object, then an object pronominal suffix is added:

Ngan-a-juba-yina

I(SUBJECT)-FUTURE-ask-him/her(OBJECT)

I will ask him/her

This word can be a complete sentence. Or it may be augmented by a free pronoun and/or a noun phrase indicating the identity of the person asked.

In some languages with bound pronouns these are all suffixes to the verb; in others they are all prefixes. A third set—to which

Nyigina belongs—has subject bound pronouns as prefixes and object ones as suffixes.

All languages—right across the world—have demonstratives, used for pointing at someone or something. There are just two in English: *this* for 'near the speaker' and *that* for 'not near the speaker'. Many Australian languages show larger systems. For instance, demonstratives in Bandjalang (spoken around the Clarence River in northern New South Wales) recognise three degrees of distance, and also show whether one is referring to one person (singular) or more than one (plural):

	near speaker	mid-distance from speaker	far from speaker
SINGULAR	gala	mala	gila
PLURAL	gaañu	maañu	gaamu

Near the beginning of chapter 1, we quoted a Bandjalang sentence: 'This dog ran', with the singular 'near speaker' demonstrative *gala*. There are in fact three ways of stating in Bandjalang that a dog (*dabaay*) ran (*gawarini*):

Gala dabaay gawarini	This dog (near me) ran
Mala dabaay gawarini	That dog (mid-distant from me) ran
Gila dabaay gawarini	That dog (far from me) ran

There is a great deal of further complication. Forms *gala*, *mala*, and *gila* are used for the subject of a verb like 'run'. For the singular subject of a verb which takes an object (such as 'take' or 'hit') one would use *galiyu*, *maliyu*, or *giliyu*. And there are different forms for 'to this/that dog' or 'from this/that dog' (in both singular and plural), and much more. Australian languages really do have intricate grammatical systems; this chapter does no more than provide a glimpse into them.

Also quoted close to the beginning of chapter 1 was a sentence from Martuthunira, the language of the nation Dampier encountered on his second visit to Western Australia, in 1699: *Nhiyu* ('this') *muyi* ('dog') *wanyjarrilha* ('ran'). Like Bandjalang, there are three sets of demonstratives. But rather than relating to three degrees of distance from the speaker, in Martuthunira they indicate whether the person or thing being pointed out is near the speaker, near the addressee, or not near either. There are separate forms for subject function and object function (and more besides):

	near me	near you	not near me or you
SUBJECT FUNCTION	nhiyu	nhula	ngunhu
OBJECT FUNCTION	yirna	nhulaa	ngumu

The Western Desert language (spoken over a million and a quarter square kilometres of arid and semi-arid country across parts of South Australia, the Northern Territory, and Western Australia) has no less than four demonstratives. Their forms in the Yankunytjatjara dialect are:

nyanga	'this very close to the speaker'
pala	'this quite close to the speaker'
nyarra	'that not near to the speaker (may or may not be visible)'
panya	'that which was referred to earlier or is remembered'

The plural suffix -*n* can be added to each of these forms to indicate reference to more than one person, animal, etc.

It is interesting that *pala* is less frequent than *nyanga* and is often used when the speaker thinks that the addressee is not really paying attention to something which is close, and directs them to notice it. The third demonstrative, *nyarra*, refers to something far away, which is not necessarily visible; the distance involved is relative and will depend on the context of the utterance—it could be 20 metres, 1 kilometre, or even 100 kilometres.

In English, *that* can be used for pointing at someone. In a store, one might say 'I'll have that', indicating what is wanted without knowing its name. It can also be employed to refer back to something just mentioned, as in:

I'll have some whisky, because that is the best remedy for a bad cold

Here, *that* refers back to *some whisky*.

Whereas in English *that* undertakes double duty, referring both to something in the situation and to something previously mentioned, the Western Desert language has a special demonstrative, *panya*, just for the latter function. It can also be used when a speaker is trying to remember something from the past and has difficulty doing so. *Panya* may be used together with the interrogative *nyaa* 'what':

Nyaa? Nyaa panya?   What (is it)? What is it, you know the one?

Just like Latin and Greek, each of the original languages of Australia has a number of case suffixes which are added to nouns and adjectives and serve to indicate their function in a sentence. This can be illustrated from Martuthunira, with the noun *muyi* 'dog'. Its forms include:

muyi	subject of a sentence; for instance, 'the dog ran' or 'the dog bit me'
muyi-i	object of a sentence; for instance, 'the snake bit the dog'
muyi-ngka	'on the dog'
muyi-ngka-nguru	'from the dog'
muyi-irta	'to the dog'

In English the possessive markers *'s* and *of* can be used (1) to describe a part of something, such as 'John's foot' or 'the leg of the table', and (2) for something which is owned and can be got rid of, such as 'John's car' or 'the dog's bone'. Australian languages have different grammatical techniques for dealing with these. Illustrating from Dyirbal:

(1) For a 'whole part' relation, the words referring to 'whole' and 'part' are simply juxtaposed, with no grammatical marking. For example:

[Nguma	dandal]_{SUBJECT}	gayñja-n
father	clavicle	break-PAST

Father's clavicle (collarbone) broke

This 'whole-part' construction is used for parts of the body of humans and animals, and for parts of artefacts (for example, the point on a spear may be called its 'nose').

(2) For a relationship of 'ownership', a possessive suffix, *-ngu*, is added to the word(s) referring to the possessor. For example:

[Nguma-ngu	wangal]_{SUBJECT}	gayñja-n
father-POSSESSIVE	boomerang	break-PAST

Father's boomerang broke

In Dyirbal, as in many other Australian languages, 'name' is treated as an inherent attribute of a person, just like a body part. *Dirra* is 'name' and father's name is simply *nguma dirra* (never *nguma-ngu dirra*).

Generally, each word in a sentence will be marked for its function in that sentence. In Dyirbal one could say:

[[Yara-ngu	jami-ngu]_{POSSESSOR}	guda]_{SUBJECT}	jinggali-ñu	[mija-gu	guñu-gu]
man-POSSESSIVE	fat-POSSESSIVE	dog	run-PAST	camp-TO	new-TO

The fat man's dog ran to the new camp

There is no suffix on *guda* 'dog' showing that it is the subject for verb *jinggaliñu* 'ran'. Both *yara* 'man' and *jami* 'fat' bear possessive suffix *-ngu*, showing that 'fat man' is the owner of the dog; *yara-ngu jami-ngu* is added to *guda* within the subject noun phrase. The dog is running *to* the new camp, thus suffix *-gu* 'to' is added to the noun *mija* 'camp' and also to its adjectival modifier *guñu* 'new'.

Since the function of each word is shown by a suffix (or the lack of a suffix for *guda*), the words may be permuted into any order and the meaning of the sentence would be unchanged. Varied word orders are common. A word which is to be focused on may be stated first, to emphasise it. Suppose that someone was told that the dog had run to a camp and asked which camp. The reply might put *guñu-gu* 'new-TO' at the beginning of the sentence; the other words could come in any order. One might hear:

Guñu-gu guda yara-ngu jinggali-ñu mija-gu jami-ngu

The fat man's dog ran to the *new* camp

Irrespective of the order in which the words are pronounced, the function of each in the sentence—and the meaning of the sentence as a whole—is clear from the suffix (or lack of suffix) on each word.

A comprehensive treatment of the grammar of any of the original languages of Australia runs to several hundred pages. It is replete with technical terms such as 'ergative', 'transitivity', 'antipassive derivation', and 'serial verb constructions'. The present chapter has provided a number of guarded peeps into this grammatical wonderland. It should be sufficient to demonstrate the communicative power of these ancient and intricate languages.

9

Remarkable genders

There are many types of things in the world. Each language will have words for referring to things which are relevant and important within the life-style of its speakers. However, one requires more than just a lengthy collection of words. They need to be grouped together, showing the way in which speakers classify the world around them.

English does this to a limited extent. The general term 'reptiles' encompasses snakes, lizards, and crocodiles; 'polygon' covers triangles, squares, rectangles, and pentagons; while spiders, scorpions, mites, and ticks are grouped together as 'arachnids'. However, one does not have to know these classificatory labels in order to speak the language efficiently. Someone can be scared of spiders without knowing that they are arachnids, or attach magical properties to triangles while being totally unaware of the word 'polygon'.

Some languages are unlike English in that categorisation is built into the grammar. They have a set of 'classifiers'; whenever a specific noun is used, in a particular context, it should be accompanied by the appropriate classifier. Classifiers can refer to inherent nature ('human', 'plant', 'cloth'), to shape ('long' or 'short', 'straight' or 'crooked'), to function ('edible', 'habitable'), and more besides.

Indonesian is a language of this type. To indicate in Indonesian how many there are of something, a speaker will generally include the appropriate classifier between number word and specific noun. Number words include *satu* 'one' (which reduces to prefix *se-* before a classifier), *dua* 'two' and *tiga* 'three' (which do not reduce). This can be illustrated with four of the several dozen classifiers, plus an example of how each is employed.

CLASSIFIER	EXAMPLE OF USE
orang 'human'	se-orang guru 'one teacher'
ekor 'living creature'	dua ekor ular 'two snakes'
beotuk 'round and curved object'	tiga beotuk galang 'three bangles'
carik 'flat thing'	se-carik kertax 'one sheet of paper'

Classifiers indicating inherent nature are *orang*, *ekor*, and also *buah* 'inanimate things'. Other classifiers referring to shape include: *batang* 'cylindrical objects such as pipes, tree trunks, and cigarettes'; *biji* 'small, round objects such as soap, cakes, eggs, grains'; and *bilah* 'sharp things such as knives and needles'.

In a number of Australian languages, many nouns are typically accompanied by an appropriate classifier. We can illustrate this for Yidiñ, spoken to the south of the present-day city of Cairns. In order to say 'the sand wallaby is standing by a black pine', a speaker of Yidiñ is likely to include the classifier *miña* 'edible animal' with the specific noun *ganguul* 'sand wallaby (*Macropus agilis*)' and classifier *jugi* 'tree' with specific noun *gubuma* 'black pine tree (*Sundacarpus amarus*)'. They would say (glossing classifiers in capital letters):

[Miña	ganguul]	jana-ng	[jugi-il	gubuma-la]
EDIBLE.ANIMAL	sand.wallaby	stand-PRESENT	TREE-LOC	black.pine-LOC

Literally: The edible-animal sand wallaby is standing by a tree black pine

Classifier *miña* and specific noun *ganguul* are grouped together as the subject noun phrase, while classifier *jugi* and specific noun *gubuma* make up the locative phrase (each of them is marked by a variant of the locative case suffix, *-il* on *jugi* and *-la* on *gubuma*).

Yidiñ has more than a dozen classifiers referring to inherent nature. Besides *jugi* 'tree', they include *waguuja* 'human male', *buña* 'human female', *jarruy* 'bird', *manggum* 'frog', *gala* 'spear' (there are several specific varieties), and *walba* 'stone'. Some of the specific nouns classified as 'stone' include:

walba malan	'flat rock'
walba bunda	'mountain'
walba burray	'cave'
walba yirriy	'type of slatey stone'

There are also half-a-dozen classifiers which relate to function and use. The most important are *miña* 'edible flesh food', *mayi* 'edible plant', and *bana* 'drinkable liquid'. Another is *bulmba* 'habitable place', illustrated in:

bulmba dugur	'house'
bulmba dabul	'beach'
bulmba buluba	'fighting ground'
bulmba burray	'cave'

Notice that *burray* 'cave' can be accompanied by classifier *walba* when its stony character is being referred to, and by *bulmba* when the focus is on a cave as a place of shelter.

For any language, the way in which words are put together is a matter of style. A speaker of Yidiñ will often, but not always, include an appropriate classifier with a specific noun. To do so in every instance would be unbearably pedantic; to never use a classifier would show one's linguistic inadequacy. The skill is to strike the right balance, taking account of genre, subject matter, and the audience.

Classifiers play a pivotal role in constructing felicitous discourse. Some Australian languages are parsimonious, typically answering a question with just 'yes' or 'no'. Yidiñ, however, is of a different ilk; a response to a question should be a full sentence, with subject and verb. But—for good style—the reply should not use exactly the same words as the question. Some variation is desirable and this is where classifiers come in useful, as in the following exchange:

QUESTION:	Ñundu	duguur-mu	gada-añ?
	you	house-FROM	come-PAST

Have you just come from the house?

ANSWER:	Ngayu	bulmba-m	gada-añ
	I	HABITABLE.PLACE-FROM	come-PAST

I have just come from the habitable place

Here the questioner just uses specific noun *dugur* (which becomes *duguur-mu* with the case suffix 'from'), not accompanied by a classifier. To produce a felicitous reply, the other speaker replaces *dugurr* wih the appropriate classifier *bulmba* 'habitable place' (with suffix *-m* 'from').

A dictionary should include relevant information concerning how to use each word. For a language with a gender system (soon to be discussed), this includes gender specification. If a language has classifiers, then classifier specification is required. And this can be a tremendous help in showing what can and what cannot be eaten.

A selection of the dictionary entries for snakes provides an illustration:

bima, 'death adder (*Acanthophis antarcticus*)'

gajamay (miña), 'brown tree snake (*Boiga irregularis*)'

gunduy, 'black snake (*Pseudechis porphryiacus*)'

wungul (miña), 'large carpet snake or python (*Morelia amethystina*)'

The inclusion of the 'edible flesh food' classifier *miña* with two of the snake names, and its omission from the other two entries, show that *gajamay* and *wungul* (not *bima* and *gunduy*) were considered edible by speakers of Yidiñ.

A further illustration can be provided for a sample of four plant names (all from the Myrtaceae family):

---

buruburu (*mayi*), 'Bamaga satin ash, water cherry (*Syzygium tierneyanum*)'

---

jurbu, 'rose gum (*Eucalyptus grandis*)'

---

wuybun, 'Moreton Bay ash, carbeen bloodwood (*Corymbia tessallaris*)'

---

yarruju (*mayi*), 'finger cherry (*Rhodomyrtus macrocarpa*)'

A glance at the dictionary shows that *buruburu* and *yarruju* are marked with 'edible plant' classifier *mayi* and can be eaten, but *jurbu* and *wuybun* are not so marked and are not considered edible.

There is another method for categorising nouns: a grammatical system of gender. Several thousand languages across the world have genders, more than have classifiers. (Just a few have both, and quite a few show neither.) Latin and German have three genders, French and Spanish just two. At the beginning of chapter 1, 'This dog ran' was illustrated for three languages. Estonian lacks genders whereas Polish and Italian each have two: masculine and feminine.

There are significant differences between classifiers and genders. First, gender is an obligatory specification; each noun must be marked for its gender. In contrast, classifiers are often optional. The number of choices in a gender system is smallish, seldom more than about eight, whereas classifier sets typically have several dozen members. In a gender language, every noun belongs to a gender class. In a classifier language there will be some nouns for which no classifier is available. In Yidiñ these include: dog (which is never eaten), grasses, boomerangs (although there are several varieties), and all body parts. Moreover, some nouns have a choice of classifier. *Yarruju* 'finger cherry' is used with classifier *mayi* 'edible plant' when its fruit are being discussed but with classifier *jugi* 'tree, wood' when talking about its timber. Another example was mentioned before: *burray*, 'cave', can be described either in terms of its being made of stone (classifier *walba*) or as a handy place to sleep (classifier *bulmba*).

The gender of a noun is always shown on some word outside the noun itself—on article, demonstrative, or modifying adjective, sometimes on the verb of the clause. In the example sentence from Italian 'This dog ran', the masculine gender of *cane* 'dog' was shown by using the masculine singular nominative form of demonstrative 'this', *questo*. Compare with the demonstative needed by a feminine noun:

MASCULINE	FEMININE
questo cane	questa volpe
'this dog'	'this fox'

In Italian all nouns are divided between these two genders. Some animals have different names for the two sexes; for example, masculine *toro* 'bull' and feminine *mucca* 'cow'. Sometimes there is just a difference in the final vowel to mark sex: masculine *asino* 'male donkey' and feminine *asina* 'female donkey'. And many nouns—such as *cane* 'dog' and *volpe* 'fox'—belong to a single gender.

Gender systems are found in several dozen of the original languages of Australia; the number of genders in the system ranges from two to eight. In some, gender is shown by an affix on the noun itself with the same affix repeated on modifying demonstratives and adjectives. In others, gender is shown through separate words.

There is a remarkable system of four genders in Dyirbal, spoken immediately to the south of Yidiñ (although there are some similarities between the languages, overall Dyirbal and Yidiñ are about as different as English and Welsh). Each noun belongs to one gender, this being shown by the form of a demonstrative-type word which accompanies it (rather like *questo* and *questa* in Italian). These are *bayi*, *balan*, *balam*, and *bala*. For example:

bayi guñjuy	'that thunderstorm'
balan buni	'that fire'
balam mirrañ	'that black bean tree'
bala diban	'that stone'

When I began work on this language, back in 1963, there was no difficulty in finding which gender class each noun belonged to. But what were the semantic principles underlying this assignment?

I made a chart of gender membership, labelling the classes I, II, III, and IV. It included:

Gender I, *bayi*	Gender II, *balan*	Gender III, *balam*	Gender IV, *bala*
men and boys	women and girls		body parts
most animals	dog		
some birds	most birds		
most snakes	some snakes		
most insects	some insects	honey	bees
moon	sun		
thunderstorm, rainbow			wind
	fire		
	water		
	fighting ground		camp, house
	some plants without edible parts	plants with edible parts	most plants without edible parts
			stone, earth language, noises, flesh food (meat and fish), etc.

It was hard to discern any rationale here. Most birds are *balan* but quite a few are *bayi*. Most snakes are *bayi* but some are *balan*. Did speakers have to learn the gender of each noun on an individual basis, without there being any general principles involved? Surely not.

As I gradually got under the skin of the language, as it were, and discussed matters with my teachers, things gradually fell into place. I found that gender assignment is based not just on the innate nature of the referent of a noun but on culturally perceived associations and oppositions, and on the beliefs and legends of the community. In essence, there appear to be a number of basic concepts associated with each gender, plus a number of principles for assigning or transferring genders.

THE BASIC CONCEPTS ARE:

I	*bayi*—male humans; non-human animates
II	*balan*—female humans; fire; drinkable liquids; fighting
III	*balam*—edible plant food
IV	*bala* is then a residue gender, dealing with everything else, including body parts, stone, earth, language, noises, and flesh food (meat and fish)

All nouns referring to an animate being are either *bayi* or *balan*, except for bees (this will soon be explained). The *balan* gender consists of four quite distinct items: (a) words for human females such as *gajin* 'girl' and *mangguy* 'woman who has lost a child'; (b) anything to do with fire, including flames, flying sparks, matches, and firesticks; (c) words referring to any liquid which may be drunk, including river, spring, lake, spray, and steam; (d) anything to do with fighting (weapons such as spears and shields), and the fighting ground itself.

Whereas there are in the world a multiplicity of things, the grammar of any language has only a limited number of parameters. Several notions may be included in a single gender, but this does not imply that there is any physical or mental connection between them. In Latin, for instance, the names of all winds and most rivers and mountains are in the same gender as names of human males. This does not imply that winds and so on are thought of as men. Not at all. It is just that this gender in Latin includes several groupings.

It would be misleading to name the *balan* gender in Dyirbal 'feminine'. This would impute female characteristics to words relating to fire, drinkable liquids and fighting, which would be quite illicit. My elderly teachers emphasised that there is no implied connection between, say, women and fire. It's just that they are both *balan*, a grammatical convenience with no bearing on their role in the world.

Augmenting the basic concepts for gender assignment, there are a number of cultural principles.

A. Gender assigned on the basis of legend and belief

The sun, *balan garri*, is believed to be a woman with the moon, *bayi gagara*, being her husband; on this basis they are assigned to the same genders as real-life women and men. The rainbow, *bayi yamani*, is a man in legend. And so is *bayi guñjuy* 'thunderstorm'. In contrast, *gulubu* 'wind' is simply placed in the residue gender, with *bala*.

Birds are believed to embody the spirits of dead women, and thus are *balan* (rather than the expected *bayi* for non-human animates). However, some individual birds have a special role in mythology and are assigned a gender depending on whether they were legendary men or women. For instance, the willy wagtail (*Rhipidura leucophrys*) is *bayi jigirrjigirr* since he is thought of as the metamorphosis of a legendary man; the way in which the bird wiggles his tail is reminiscent of how men dance in a corroboree. Most insects are, as expected, *bayi* but I was told that crickets and grasshoppers are regarded as 'old ladies' and are thus *balan*.

B. Gender assigned on the basis of physical association

The *balam* gender is simplest of all, dealing just with plants with some edible fruit or nut or root or bulb. It also includes *balam girñjal* 'honey', since this is made from the nectar of flowers. Fruit (*balam*) comes from trees (*bala*) and honey (*balam*) comes from bees. For this reason bees are in the *bala* gender, like trees.

Most other insects are *bayi*, the gender for non-human animates. But the firefly, *balan yugiyam*, is *balan* because the flashes of light it emits are similar to sparks from a fire (although they are not hot).

C. Gender assignment to highlight an important property

If a set of nouns has gender X, and a subset has some particular property, then this subset may be assigned a gender other than X. Three kinds of important property have been identified.

- **Can be eaten.** Pythons (or carpet snakes) are typically eaten by speakers of Dyirbal. They are thus *balan*, to distinguish them from other snakes which are almost all *bayi*.

- **What they eat.** Whereas most birds are *balan*, and are included under the generic term *balan dundu*, birds of prey are not covered by *balan dundu* and are given gender marker *bayi*. I was told that this is because 'they eat *dundu*'. Some (but not all) birds of prey have a role as men in legends, this providing a second reason for their being *bayi*; for example, *bayi gurrijala* 'eaglehawk (*Aquela audax*)'.

- **Being harmful to humans.** There are four plants, all in the Urticacae family, which are *balan* because of their harmful property—if a leaf is stroked in the wrong direction, the hairs on it will inflict a sting that persists for months. Two are stinging trees, *balan dungan* (*Dendrocnide moriodes*) and *balan giyarra* (*D. photinophylla*) and two are stinging vines, *balan bumbilan* (*Urtica incisa*) and *balan binggilgayi* (*Tragia novahollandiae*).

The basic concepts and the three principles do provide an explanation for almost all instances of gender assignment in Dyirbal. But not quite for all of them. For example, no reason was forthcoming for why *guda* 'dog' should be *balan*.

I have shown that the semantic basis of gender in Dyirbal is not simply taxonomic, but involves principles for transferring gender membership, and that an understanding of it depends on a close cultural knowledge—the people's repertoire of beliefs and legends.

In chapter 5 attention was drawn to the different referents of kinship terms between languages. In English, *son* is used for a male child and *daughter* for a female one, of both mother and father. In Dyirbal *daman* is used for all children of mother (also used by her siblings) and *galbin* for all children of father (also used by his siblings). Adding gender markers, four kinds of children are distinguished:

bayi daman 'mother's son'	bayi galbin 'father's son'
balan daman 'mother's daughter'	balan galbin 'father's daughter'

This shows that having a gender marker on each noun means that a language needs fewer lexical words. In Dyirbal *bilmbu* is used for any person who has lost their spouse. Gender then distinguishes *balan bilmbu* 'widow' and *bayi bilmbu* 'widower'.

Gender plays an especially important role in the mother-in-law avoidance style, Jalnguy (described in chapter 6), which typically has a single word corresponding to several in the everyday speech style. For example, the rainbow (a most important spirit) is *bayi yamani* in the everyday style and *bayi gagilbarra* in Jalnguy. The wompoo pigeon (*Ptilinopus magnificus*) is given the same name in Jalnguy as the rainbow since its colour is like the green of the rainbow. The flame kurrajong tree (*Brachychiton acerifolius*) is held to be sacred to the rainbow snake, and is similarly named. But contrastive gender markers serve to distinguish the three items.

	IN EVERYDAY STYLE	IN JALNGUY STYLE
rainbow	bayi yamani	bayi gagilbarra
wompoo pigeon	balan bagamu	balan gagilbarra
flame kurrajong	bala dila	bala gagilbarra

When considering the set of classifiers in Yidiñ, it was seen that the inclusion of the appropriate classifier in the dictionary entry for a noun showed whether or not it was considered edible. This was illustrated with four names for trees, only two of which were classified as *mayi* 'edible plant'.

Dyirbal works in the same way for plants: gender marker *balam* indicates that a part of the plant can be eaten, while *bala* shows the contrary, as in entries for the same four trees from the Myrtaceae family (notice that names for the trees in Yidiñ and in Dyirbal are quite different):

marraja, balam, 'Bamaga satin ash, water cherry (*Syzygium tierneyanum*)'

yagirra, bala, 'rose gum (*Eucalyptus grandis*)'

jinjila, bala, 'Moreton Bay ash, carbeen bloodwood (*Corymbia tessallaris*)'

gaynggal, balam, 'finger cherry (*Rhodomyrtus macrocarpa*)'

(In fact, the ending -*m* on edible gender marker *balam* in Dyirbal probably emanates from a classifier *mayi* in an earlier stage of the language. A sequence of *bala* 'that' plus *mayi* could have reduced to become *balam*.)

The Yidiñ dictionary also indicates which living things are considered edible through including classifier *miña* 'edible non-flesh food'. There is nothing comparable in Dyirbal. For instance, some grubs are eaten, whereas others are regarded as inedible, but all bear gender marker *bayi*. There is no way of telling, from the dictionary, that speakers of Dyirbal eat *bayi jambun* 'long wood grub' and *bayi gabun* 'small grub found in an acacia tree' but not *bayi gayñjim* 'a grub that lives in rotten wood' or *bayi gurruburr* 'a green grub found on the leaves of a cocky apple tree'. (Note that Yidiñ and Dyirbal dictionaries are both more informative than those for English, a language which has no classifiers and no genders (apart from sex-based pronouns *he*, *she*, and *it*). As a consequence, English dictionaries do not automatically provide information concerning which plants and animals are considered edible.)

The gender system in Dyirbal reflects the ways in which its speakers view the world. Classifiers in Yidiñ fulfil a quite different role, showing how to live in the world.

We can now move on to an examination of the rich vocabularies of Australian languages, illustrating the precision of naming and the subtle meaning distinctions which reflect life-style, habits of social interaction, and mental attitudes.

10

Oodles of words

Each of the original languages of Australia has a robust vocabulary with thousands of nouns, verbs, and adjectives. Meanings attached to words reflect the exigencies of daily life in the environment in which the language is spoken.

For a language spoken in the lush rainforest of the north-east coast—amid cascading rivers and waterfalls—it is natural to specify where something is in terms of upriver or downriver or across a river. In desert regions of Western Australia, sources of water (*kapi*) are few and are remembered. Travellers must reach a waterhole each night, with the word *kapi* having a secondary meaning, 'camp'. 'The distance or the number of days' journey between two places is the number of *kapi*, which are usually enumerated by name in association with the joints of the fingers.'

In their everyday style of speaking, the original inhabitants of Australia abhorred vagueness. If a statement can be made explicitly, then so it should be. In Dyirbal, for instance, there is no verb 'know'. If you know something then you must say what you know and how you know it. Whereas in English one might say—vaguely and elusively—'I know where the bull-roarer is', a speaker of Dyirbal has to be more specific. They might say: 'The bull-roarer is in the hollow tree', and also indicate how this is known—for instance 'I saw it there' or 'My father told me it is there'.

There are several ways of responding 'I don't know', depending on the nature of the question. If asked about a location, 'Where's the bull-roarer?' or 'Where is your father?' one would say *Juru* 'I don't know'. A negative reply to other kinds of questions, such as 'What's the name of that person/place?' or 'What happened?' or 'What did the old man do?' would be *Ngañum* 'I don't know'.

There is precision in naming, with a distinct label for every variety of tree, fern, and vine, every type of animal, fish, and insect. And also for parts of the body. For example, here are some of the names for bones in Dyirbal:

dandal	clavicle	collarbone
birumba	scapula	shoulderblade
gubaguba	sternum	breast bone
wanggirr	costae verae	true ribs
ngiyar	costae spuriae	false ribs
bilumba	ilium	hip bone
gumbun	coccyx	tail bone
manggu	radius	bigger bone in lower arm
girman	ulna	smaller bone in lower arm
giyañ	patella	knee cap
dujul	tibia	bigger bone in lower leg
jijal	fibula	smaller bone in lower leg

Many speakers of English would be familiar with few—or none—of the technical designations in the middle column, contenting themselves with the descriptive labels from the right-hand side.

Dyirbal also has names for the various varieties of muscles, including *waju* for the trapezius muscle (over the back of the neck and the shoulder), *ngawun* for the deltoid muscle (over the shoulder joint)—also used for the muscle in a bird's wing, by which it flies—*wangun* for the gluteus muscles (in the buttocks), and *ruba* for the gastrocernius muscle (inside the calf).

Body part terms in Australian languages are extended to describe features of animals, of artefacts, of plants, and of the environment. For example, in Dyirbal the central meaning of *guwu* is 'nose' and to this is added a range of secondary senses:

body parts	nipple on breast
	glans penis (end part, usually covered by the foreskin)
	beak of a bird
artefacts	pointed end of a spear
	end of the barrel on a gun
	operative end of a firestick
	prow of a canoe
	hand of a clock
	bumper bar on a car
	pointed end of a sign made by the roadside, indicating direction to go
environment	peak of a mountain

The large flightless cassowary (*Casuarius casuarius*), *gunduy*, is both an unusual and an important creature. There are special terms for its distinctive body parts:

yiñji	feathers (contrasting with the general term for feathers, *yila*)
barrambi	casque (or 'helmet') on top of the head
yirrgun	neck (whereas the general term for neck is *gurrga*)
gurgaji	red wattles hanging down from the front of the neck
birambiram	rump (where the feathers come out)
burrabur	the fat inside a cassowary (the general term for fat is *jami*)
wuybali	large claw on the back foot of a cassowary, with which it kicks and inflicts injury; this term is also used for the back claw of a platypus (which injects poison), the tail of a blue-tongue lizard, and a type of short, thick spear

Most, but not all, features of implements are described through extensions of body part terms. Consider, for instance, names in Dyirbal for parts of the boomerang, *wangal*:

- the end by which the boomerang is held, to be thrown, is *mulu*; this is the general term for 'end', of a log, a piece of string, a road, a swamp, etc.; it is not a body part term
- the other end is *jina* 'foot'
- the outside curve is *buru* 'elbow'
- the inside curve is *bamba* 'stomach'.

Extension of meaning for a body part can carry over into the sacred domain. For instance, in Yolngu, from eastern Arnhem Land, the noun *rlikan* denotes 'elbow' and also:

plant	branch of a tree joining its trunk
environment	bay between two promontories
religion/ritual	clan designs and sacred paintings
	'power' names of a clan's sacred objects

It is unusual to encounter an extension of meaning in the other direction, with a body part being described in terms of, say, an artefact. Rare examples include 'neck-boomerang' for collarbone in Yir-Yoront (from the western part of the Cape York Peninsula) and 'mouth-boomerang' for jaw bone in Diyari (from northern South Australia).

When working on Yidiñ, I encountered *bunggu* as the name for 'knee'. A straightforward body part term? Not at all. Gradually, the full semantic import of this word came to be revealed. *Bunggu* is also used to describe a wave in the sea and I put this down to shape similarity. It is used in this language for the outside bend on a boomerang. And for the bend in the body of a snake as it moves along the ground. Again, from the Anglocentric viewpoint of 'knee' as the main meaning and the other senses as metaphorical extensions, I regarded the 'boomerang' and 'snake' senses as being based on similarity of shape. But one day my elderly teacher remarked—in English—that a car had a 'flat knee'. 'Wheel' is also called *bunggu* and he was transferring the Yidiñ range of meaning into English. Eventually, I worked out that *bunggu* has a basic general meaning 'that part of a body whose movement is the major factor in propelling the entire body (along the ground, or through the air, or across the water)'. In keeping with this, *bunggu* is also used metaphorically for a 'turn' in singing, someone taking over the singing of a song part-way through; it is this movement that keeps the song going.

Across the original cultures of Australia, the ear is held to be the seat of intelligence and understanding. Anyone who is smart and clever is said to have a 'good ear'. The most extreme way of denigrating a man's intellect may be to liken their ear to female genitalia. Descriptions of mental states are often based on the word 'ear'. This can be illustrated from Guugu Yimidhirr (the language which James Cook encountered in 1770) where *milga* is 'ear' and based on it we find:

milga-dhirr	(ear-WITH)	'obedient'
milga-mul	(ear-WITHOUT)	'disobedient, stupid, deaf'
milga ngamba	(ear unaware)	'careless, heedless, won't listen to anything'
milga dhundal	(ear soft/wet)	'be sorry, homesick, missing someone'
milga ngandal	(ear refuse)	'forget, fail to heed'
milga ngalburr	(ear enclose)	'be absorbed in something'
milga biinii	(ear dry.up)	'obsessed, compulsive'
milga bubu	(ear earth)	'thick-skinned, insensitive, can't be insulted'

In some languages, verbs for 'smell' and 'taste' are based on 'hear'. For example, one might say, literally, 'smoke-hear' to describe smelling something which is smoking. In Dyirbal the reflexive form of verb *ngamba-n* 'hear, listen to' is used for 'think': *ngamba-yirri-ñu*, literally 'listen to oneself'.

Words describing bodily actions and states may be based on a variety of body part terms. A sample from Yir-Yoront is:

'nose stand' for 'sneeze'

'nose carry' for 'snore'

'teeth throw' for 'whistle'

'throat buzz' for 'burp'

'mouth break' for 'yawn'

'eye throw' for 'wait and worry'

However, other languages have separate words (not involving body part nouns) for these activities.

Each group of people needs a specialised vocabulary to describe activities that are central to their style of living. Australians typically have a range of verbs for different modes of spearing. For example, the spear may be held in the hand or thrown. If thrown, this may be directly from the hand or by means of a woomera—a stick onto which the spear is latched, to provide greater propulsion (somewhat like an extra joint to the arm). If the spear is held in the hand, it may be directed at something which can be seen or at some possible target which is unseen: 'blind spearing' among submerged tree roots in the hope that an eel may be hiding there, or into long grass where movement has been detected, suggesting an animal within.

Social interaction is of paramount importance in every society. English has a number of semi-synonyms for the verb *ask*, including *request*, *solicit*, and *enquire* (also spelled *inquire*). Australian languages show a rather different range of meanings. This can be illustrated from Dyirbal (the language which I know best):

nganban	the general term 'ask'; for example, ask where someone is, ask for matches
nginggin	ask for food (typically used of a child, or a bird chick with open mouth)
ngibañu	ask someone to do a certain thing; for example, fetch some firewood
yumban	ask someone to come over to visit you
bunman	ask someone to accompany you
gurrngalman	entreat someone to go with you after they have initially refused (even though they generally do accompany you)
guñjiñu	keep on asking a question when you've already been given an answer

In many languages, the same word can be used for both an object and some notable characteristic of it, or for an act associated with it. English is particularly rich in this respect—noun *skin* can also be used as a verb 'remove the skin from something'; *butter* is primarily a noun but also a verb 'spread butter—or something similar, such as margarine—on'; *silver* as a noun describes a metal, and it is also an adjective referring to the colour of the metal.

Australian languages often have a word which refers to both some actual thing or activity, and also its potential. Many languages have distinct terms for 'wood' and 'fire' but in others there is just one word covering both; wood has the potential to make a fire. There is typically a single term for 'edible animal' (what it is) and 'meat' (what it can become).

If an artefact is preferentially manufactured from a certain tree, then the same name may be given to both. This can be illustrated for the fire-making apparatus in Dyirbal. It consists of:

bagu	the bottom portion: a flat piece of wood with a shallow hole in it
jiman	a hardwood stick which is twirled between the hands, pressing an end down into the hole in the bottom portion, the *bagu*, producing sparks which ignite dried grass or a dry leaf by the hole

Jiman is also the name for the whole apparatus.

The *bagu* is typically made from *bubarrila*, 'milky pine tree (*Alstonia scholaris*)'. This is hung in smoke over a fire to dry and then wrapped in leaves to keep dry. The vertical stick, *jiman*, is the more important component, and must be made from a very hard timber. The preferred tree is the tetra beech (*Steganthera laxiflora*), and this is also called *jiman*.

If this tree is not available, there are a number of alternatives. One is another tetra beech, the closely related *Wilkiea pubescenes*. This is called *jiman-jiman*, the doubling of *jiman* in its name indicating similarity to the preferred tree, *jiman*. If neither of these is available, it is possible to use the bush guava (*Eupomatia laurina*); this has a quite different name, *muja*.

The actual/potential conflation may extend to verbs. For instance, in some—but by no means all—languages, the same word can cover both 'seek, look for' and 'find'. Isn't this confusing, you might ask? Not at all. The sense intended is made clear by the sentential context. In present tense the meaning is 'seek' ('I am seeking it') and in past tense it is likely to be 'find' (that is, 'I successfully sought it'). A statement that you had unsuccessfully sought something could be 'I sought it all day yesterday but didn't see it'.

We also find, in some languages, a verb referring to a certain action irrespective of whether it is performed volitionally or non-volitionally. For instance, 'fall down (involuntarily)' and 'throw oneself to the ground (perhaps to avoid a missile)' may be two senses of a single verb. The context of speaking will show which sense is relevant in a particular instance.

There are languages which have a single verb covering both 'hide (something)', which is volitional, and 'lose (something)', which isn't. Dyirbal uses separate words for these notions but Jalnguy (the avoidance or 'mother-in-law' style) does mix together acts which are purposeful with others that are accidental. Chapter 6 described how several words in the everyday style may be rendered by a single word in Jalnguy. An example of this is:

It can be seen that the Jalnguy verb *ñañjun* has a general meaning something like 'be not paying attention to (volitionally or non-volitionally)'. It covers two verbs where the subject controls the activity—*mijun* 'take no notice of' and *bujilmban* 'don't care about, completely ignore'—and also two describing something which can't be helped—*wulayman* 'lose' and *ngajin* 'forget'. (As an interesting aside, in order to say 'wait' in Dyirbal, one uses the reflexive form of *mijun* 'take no notice'—*mijuyirriñu* literally 'take no notice of oneself'.)

Some lexical notions are universal; all languages of the world have words for 'jump' and 'swim', 'sit' and 'stand', 'laugh' and 'cry'. Others are culture specific. The original peoples of Australia had no use for concepts such as 'appoint' or 'dismiss', just as the English did not need a word for 'throw a spear with the aid of a woomera'.

In Dyirbal there are adjectives *maymbi* 'can't climb trees' and *jurun* 'can't swim'. There could be similar words in English but they would be little used since such negative qualities are held to be of small importance (and anyway it might be considered impolite to draw attention to them).

However, for some words in Australian languages an English equivalent would be handy. For instance, there is often a noun for the noise when you can hear that people are talking but can't quite make out the words (this is *mulgu* in Dyirbal and *ñurrugu* in Yidiñ).

When speaking English, I often wish that we had an equivalent of the Yidiñ verb *jugaarrbang*. This describes not being able to sleep at night because your mind cannot relax. And also, in the daytime, when your mind is jumping all over the place so that you can't think straight and are unable to focus it on some particular thing (described by a bilingual speaker as 'having a fuzzy head'). *Jugaarrbang* could be translated as 'have unsettled mind' but really this provides a poor characterisation of its meaning span.

There are a myriad things, concepts, and contrasts in the world at large. A language has a finite vocabulary and grammar, so it is only able to characterise a portion of what there is outside. Each language employs a slightly different technique. For example, in English (as in other well-known languages of Europe), the adjective *new* has two meanings. One might hear a conversation such as:

Fred:	John has just bought a new car.
Jean:	Really, I didn't think he had that much money.
Frank	Oh, not a brand-new car. Just an ancient old thing, but it's new for him.

There would be no confusion if this exchange were conducted in Dyirbal, which has two adjectives corresponding to English *new*:

milgir	'brand new (just made, never been used before; for example, a shield or a boomerang)'
guñu	'new to me (perhaps a gift from someone else, after they had used it)'

There is a further sense for *guñu*: 'be rejuvenated, as when someone spruces themselves up, to look younger'.

Australian languages have a plentiful stock of adjectives dealing with human feelings. In Dyirbal, for example, we find:

gulngan	a good person: respectful, kind-hearted, grateful; for example, young people bringing water and firewood for old people
yaruyaru	easy to get on with, willing, kind, generous, obedient; for example, someone who will do anything for you (and they'll do it at once, not waiting until tomorrow), tell you anything you want to know, give you anything you ask for

gambuy	'getting over it' (naturally, or make oneself calm down); for example, cooling down after an argument; feeling sorry and contrite after committing a crime; getting over a period of sadness or worry (for example, lost lover, deceased relative)
guyngay	offended because of some slight, and now when people try to remedy it, refusing; for example, not offered something at the appropriate time, and now, when it is belatedly offered, won't accept it

Anthropologist Fred Myers discussed adjective *kunta* in the Pintupi dialect of the Western Desert language. It is defined in the Pintupi dictionary as 'shy, respectful' but is most frequently explained by bilingual speakers in terms of 'shame'. Myers lists some of the situations in which it is used:

- Someone's feelings if they are seen to do something which is poor etiquette, ill-mannered, or wrong.
- The timidity felt by young men at a public occasion that is likely to prevent their speaking out in front of older men.
- The shyness felt by children which makes them hide behind a parent in the presence of strangers.
- The awkwardness felt in the presence of strangers or people who are only distant kin which inhibits one from asking them for food or favours.
- The obligatory respect felt towards tabooed kin which necessitates avoidance of direct contact with them.
- The embarrassment felt at the use of crude language in inappropriate contexts.

The last few chapters have provided glimpses into the sound systems, grammars, and vocabularies of the 250 or so original languages of Australia. We can now turn to investigation of possible genetic relationships, both between these languages and with those spoken elsewhere.

11

Are there any language links?

Every language is in a continual state of flux. With each succeeding generation, a sprinkling of new words is introduced and some old ones cast aside. Habits of pronunciation and grammar shift. A language may at one time be spoken over several communities, each with a slightly different dialect (but still mutually intelligible). The communities then move apart, lose contact with one another, and develop in individual ways to the extent that they become distinct languages, no longer mutually intelligible. However, by comparing the words and structures in each modern language, a linguist is able to prove that they are genetically related and that they constitute one 'language family', each being a descendant of a common ancestor language. Linguists call this the 'proto-language' for the family. A good deal of the nature of the proto-language can be reconstructed, and also the systematic changes through which each of the modern languages developed from it.

Consider three familiar languages from Western Europe. This is how they say 'tree':

FRENCH	arbre
SPAINISH	árbol
ITALIAN	albero

Thousands of other words have similar form, and there are many parallels in grammar, showing that these languages (plus Portuguese, Catalan, Rumanian, and a handful more) belong to a single family, the Romance family; that is, they all descend from a common ancestor. In this instance we have written records of the mother language—it was Latin, spoken a couple of thousand years ago.

The word for 'tree' in Latin was *arbor*. Notice that it is not exactly the same as the form in any of the modern languages. They have all changed, but in different ways. (In Italian, for instance, the first *r* has shifted to *l* in order to avoid having two *r*-sounds in the same word.)

We can show the genetic relationship between these languages by a 'tree diagram':

This is rather like a genealogical diagram for kinship relations, except then we must have two parents (mother and father) at the top, whereas a genetic diagram for languages has a single 'parent', the proto-language.

To the north, we find strong resemblances between Swedish, English, and German. Consider their words for 'brother':

SWEDISH	**broder**
ENGLISH	**brother**
GERMAN	**Bruder**

Again, there are a myriad other similarities in vocabulary, phonology (sound system), and grammar, showing that these three languages (and a dozen more) belong to what is called the Germanic family. It can be diagrammed:

In this instance, there are no records of the putative ancestor language, called proto-Germanic. This would have been spoken at about the same time as Latin, but the habit of writing had not yet reached that far north.

By careful consideration of the systematic correspondences between sounds in cognate sets, such as that for 'brother', linguists have reconstructed what proto-Germanic must have been like. For instance, 'brother' is inferred to have been *brōthar* (linguists use the * symbol to indicate that the form is not known from written records, but is a reconstruction). On the basis of this, the systematic way in which each modern language developed can be understood. (No language is exactly the same as the proto-language; each has changed in a variety of ways.)

The scientific methodology of comparative linguistics allows us to range even further into the past. Let's compare the word for 'brother' in English and in languages for which we have the oldest written records: Greek and Latin, from around two thousand years in the past; and Sanskrit, spoken a few centuries earlier:

SANSKRIT	bhrātar
GREEK	phātēr
LATIN	frāter
ENGLISH	brother

The differences are greater than those for the Romance and Germanic sets just given, but we can perceive enough similarity to suggest a common genetic origin. This is borne out by many other cognate sets. The initial segment of 'brother' is different in each language. This is reconstructed as *bh for the common ancestor, proto-Indo-European. Sanskrit has retained the bh (a b with a puff of air after it) whereas the other languages have modified bh into ph, f, and b respectively. (There are a fair number of other words with this 'correspondence set' bh–ph–f–b between the four languages, showing that the matching is quite regular.)

We are here dealing with the large Indo-European language family which has a dozen branches (or sub-families) including Germanic, Romance, Celtic (Welsh, Irish, and others), Balto-Slavic (Latvian, Lithuanian, Russian, Polish, and more), Greek, Albanian, and Indo-Iranian (Persian, Sanskrit, Hindi, plus a further twenty or so languages). By systematic comparison of cognate words across all twelve branches, quite a lot has been reconstructed of the phonology, grammar, and vocabulary of the putative parent language, proto-Indo-European.

Inferences concerning relationships between languages, the details of the proto-language, and its likely date, become more tentative the further one reaches back in time. For example, proto-Indo-European is thought to have been spoken around 6,000 years ago, but individual scholars' estimates vary by a thousand years or more each side of this.

Modern humankind (*Homo sapiens*) is believed to have evolved 120,000 years ago (maybe even earlier). A defining characteristic of the species is that from the start there would have been recognisable languages. It would only have taken a handful of millennia for the languages to have attained a level of sophistication and complexity similar to that encountered across the world today.

Many questions remain unanswered. Did language evolve just once (so that the several thousand modern languages go back to a single ancient ancestor)? Or did it evolve in several places and at several times? There is absolutely no way of knowing.

It would be satisfying to be able to chronicle the stages of evolution of human languages from the earliest times to the present—the split of the dialects of one language into several distinct languages, mergers when population fell due to scarcity of water or food, contact between neighbouring people resulting in 'borrowing' of sounds, words, and structural features. Sadly, rather little is possible.

All we have to go on is the data from modern languages, together with written records of some languages spoken just a few millennia ago. And reconstructions of past proto-languages based on this modern material. The vital question is: how far can one reconstruct back?

The answer depends on a number of factors, a principal one being the rate at which the languages have changed (this does vary a good deal). Taking everything into consideration, scholars of comparative linguistics consider that the limit of reconstruction is between 5,000 and 8,000 years (depending on the circumstances).

As individual languages evolve, over time, away from the proto-language, each changes in its own way so that the similarities between them—which enable one to discern a genetic connection—gradually become less evident. This happens slowly and steadily until, after 5,000–8,000 years, one can no longer tell that the languages do go back to a common ancestor.

As a consequence, what happened between the first stages of human language(s)—120,000 years or so in the past—and the situation 8,000 or 5,000 years ago remains a mystery. *Homo sapiens* evolved in Africa and some groups are thought to have migrated into the Near East and Europe around 90,000 years before the present (BP). There is a lengthy time gap between that move and the date of the earliest reconstructed proto-languages—around 6,000 years for proto-Indo-European and similar or later dates for other families of the area: Uralic (including Finnish and Hungarian), Semitic (featuring Hebrew and Arabic), and Turkic.

It took a long time for humankind to extend to faraway places. Most islands in the Pacific were only reached within the last three millennia. Indeed, the Māori came to New Zealand only around a thousand years ago. The largest family in the world, in terms of number of languages (around 1,000) and geographical extent, is undoubtedly Austronesian. Accepted opinion is that it evolved no earlier than 6,000 BP (about the same time-depth as Indo-European), either in south China or in Taiwan. Austronesian languages then spread across Taiwan, the Philippines, Malaysia,

Indonesia, Borneo, across to Madagascar, to the coastal regions of New Guinea, then right across the Pacific as far as Hawai'i and Easter Island.

The first people to enter the Americas came across the Bering Strait from Siberia, around 12,000 BP (it could have been a little earlier, but not much). From this beginning there evolved the hundreds of modern languages across North America and an even greater number south of Panama. Historical reconstruction is necessarily 'bottom-up', commencing with the languages spoken today (there are no historical records extending back more than a few hundred years). It has been possible to recognise some dozens of language families, including Algonquian, Iroquoian, and Uto-Aztecan in North America, and Arawak, Carib, and Tupi in South America. Each of their proto-languages was spoken a few thousand years back (much less than 12,000 years). The information available does not permit us to reconstruct any further into the past. It is of course *possible* that proto-Algonquian and proto-Uto-Aztecan were related within an earlier family tree (almost nothing is impossible). But, working in terms of the scientific methodology of comparative linguistics, no proper evidence can be provided to support such a hypothesis, or any similar one.

Let us now turn to Australia, the focus of this book. But it is not just Australia which must be considered. From about 125,000 BP, New Guinea and Australia, including Tasmania, constituted a single land mass. The coastline—and the extent of land bridges between present-day New Guinea and Australia—did vary somewhat as climatic conditions shifted. But it was all one land mass until seas came between mainland Australia and Tasmania around 11,000 BP. Finally, the last land link between New Guinea and Australia—at what is now the Torres Strait—was submerged about 7,000 BP.

Archaeologists tell us that the first humans came into New Guinea/Australia no later than 50,000 BP, maybe earlier. (Dates of this order have been obtained from excavations all over the land mass.) These people presumably came from Indonesia or somewhere nearby. We cannot tell whether there was just one incursion—which could have been on the coast of what is now Australia, or on that of New Guinea—or several, perhaps at a number of places around the combined coastline.

The time-depth here is three or four times more than that for the Americans' movement over the Bering Strait. And that date is far enough in the past for it to be impossible to reconstruct a single proto-American-Indian ancestor language. Fifty thousand years is far, far longer than the accepted dates for proto-languages of any of the established families (Indo-European, Austronesian, and so on).

It is thus absolutely clear that nothing can be inferred concerning the language(s) of the first peoples to make New Guinea/Australia their home. However (as in the Americas), by comparison of the details of modern languages, some small genetic families can be recognised, such that all languages within them developed from a common ancestor a few hundred or a few thousand years in the past.

Linguist Geoffrey O'Grady suggested that nine languages from the Pilbara region of Western Australia are genetically linked in what he called the 'Ngayarda family'. (They include Martuthunira, the language Dampier encountered on his second visit to the Western Australian coast.) Employing the established 'comparative method', which had been developed for Indo-European language, O'Grady provided a convincing reconstruction of the phonology of proto-Ngayarda.

The method can be illustrated by quoting a fragment of his work. Let us compare five cognate sets in two of the languages:

	NGARLUMA	YIÑTJIIPARNTI	
1	parnrta	parnrta	creek bank
2	kapun	kawun	skin
3	papa	pawa	water
4	warpa	warwa	far
5	mirna-warra	mirna-warra	bye-and-bye

We can now examine four correspondences within these cognate sets:

	NGARLUMA	YIÑTJIIPARNTI	position in word	in cognate sets
A	p	p	initial	1, 3
B	p	w	medial	2, 3, 4
C	w	w	initial	4
D	w	w	medial	5

There are a number of other cognate sets showing each of these correspondences.

The question to answer is: in correspondence B, did proto-Ngayarda have *p or did it have *w? There are two alternatives:

(1) Proto-Ngayarda had *p. This stayed the same in Ngarluma but in Yiñtjiiparnti:

*p stayed as p in initial position

*p became w in medial position

This is a plausible scenario.

(2) Proto-Ngayarda had *w. But how then could we explain medial *w becoming *p in some words (cognate sets 2 and 3) but remaining w in others (set 5), for Ngarluma? There is no rationale for this.

Thus, O'Grady reconstructed the proto-form for 2 'skin' as *kapun*, that for 3 'water' as *papa*, and that for 4, 'far' as *warpa*.

We have examined just a microcosm of O'Grady's sophisticated reconstruction. Ngarluma has been shown to be the same as proto-Ngayarda with respect to *p in medial position; however, it differs in other respects. Overall, every one of the nine languages in the small Ngayarda family has changed in some way from the proto-language, as is always the case. O'Grady's work shows that these languages do constitute one genetic family.

Reconstruction of the grammar for a proto-language can be illustrated for a small family which consists of just two languages—Jabugay and Yidiñ—spoken to the north and south, respectively, of the present-day city of Cairns. These languages have almost identical systems of phonemes, they share about 53 per cent vocabulary, and have comparable grammatical structures. Overall, they are about as similar—or as different—as are Spanish and Italian.

Consider verbal suffixes (word endings) for the two languages: tenses, imperative (used in commands); and purposive (covering 'need', 'want', and 'in order to') for one of the conjugations. The symbol 'ø' indicates a 'zero' affix; that is, just the plain verb root is used.

	JABUGAY	YIDIÑ
imperative	ø	ø
past	-ñ	-lñu
present	-l	
future	-lna	-l
purposive	-lung	-lna

By comparison of these forms, the proto-system can be reconstructed as:

	PROTO-JABUGAY/YIDIÑ
imperative	*ø
past	*-lñu
present	*-l
future	*-lna
purposive	*-lung

In Yidiñ, the purposive has dropped out of use, with future moving over to take on its meanings, and the present tense suffix, -l, has consequently extended its range to also cover future time. In Jabugay, past tense suffix -lñu has shortened to become just -ñ. The final vowel was dropped and then the preceding -lñ- had to be abbreviated to a single consonant since neither language allows a sequence of two consonants at the end of a word.

Examining all of the 250 or so original languages of Australia, we find that about three dozen small languages families—like Ngayarda and Jabugay/Yidiñ—can be recognised, the number of languages in each family ranging from two to seventeen. And there are also a fair number of 'isolates', languages for which no genetic link with another language can be established (like Basque in Europe). There is not enough evidence to link together these small families (just as there is not enough to link proto-Iroquoian with proto-Algonquian in North America, nor proto-Indo-European with proto-Turkic in Europe).

There are around a thousand languages in New Guinea. About three hundred of these, spoken around the coast, belong to the widespread Austronesian family, and arrived within the last three or four thousand years. (There are no Austronesian languages in Australia.) The c. 700 non-Austronesian languages are called 'Papuan', which is merely a geographical label. A similar situation prevails for Papuan languages as in Australia: several dozen smallish language families have been recognised—and there are also a number of isolates—but no reputable genetic linkage can be established between the families.

(Little is known of the original languages of Tasmania—there appears to have been a policy of 'shoot first, ask questions later'. But in view of the 11,000 years of separation from the Australian mainland, no discernible genetic links would be likely.)

Once people enter an unoccupied land, they soon spread out to cover every liveable portion. It has been estimated that, in some situations, if sufficient food and land is available the population will double each generation. Dialects of a language will move apart and split to become separate languages. For the first few thousand years, genetic links would still be discernible and a genetic family tree could be constructed. But after that, and for the remainder of the 50,000 years, there would just be a patchwork of languages (displaying no overreaching genetic associations).

As water and other resources contract, population must fall. Groups will merge, with some languages being lost. When things improve, there will be expansion. The population increases, with dialect split and the creation of the many small language families we find today, such as Ngayarda and Jabugay/Yidiñ.

When a group of languages—whether all from one genetic family or from several families—have been in contiguity for some time within a geographical region, they will tend to become similar to one another in certain ways. Features are borrowed, although the languages remain distinct (that is to say, not mutually intelligible). They may have the same type of sound structure, or of verb structure, or of subordinate clauses. We say that they have a similar 'typology'. This is a quite different matter from genetic linkage. For example, Hebrew clearly belongs to the Semitic family but it has in recent years had contact with Indo-European languages with the result that it shares a number of typological features with them, such as ways of marking possession.

Linguist Arthur Capell recognised a typological distinction within Australia. About sixty languages across the north have prefixes as well as suffixes. (They include Nyigina, whose prefixes and suffixes were illustrated in chapter 8.) The remaining languages have just suffixes, no prefixes. Capell's non-prefixing group was renamed 'Pama-Nyungan' (after the words for 'man' in the extreme north-east and south-west of the continent), and criteria for this group have been modified in minor ways.

The important point is that Pama-Nyungan is simply a typological assemblage, not a genetic family. There is an established methodology for linguistic reconstruction, which is the basis for the recognition of Indo-European, Algonquian, Turkic, Austronesian, and others as genetic families. O'Grady applied these methods to the small Ngayarda family. There is no way in which, following this methodology, a proto-Pama-Nyungan language could be reconstructed.

However, not everyone abides by the rules of the game. Some, with more imagination than acumen, have assigned genetic status to 'Pama-Nyungan'. Others copy this designation. Of proof there is none, nor can there be. And why stop there? One hears talk of 'proto-Australian', spoken 50,000 or more years ago. But, if this were possible, it would surely have to be 'proto-New Guinea/ Australian'. Enough said.

How about genetic links between the original languages of Australia and those spoken elsewhere? When the first people ventured onto the New Guinea/Australia land mass, they would have left behind—in South-East Asia—relatives speaking related languages. However, that was 50,000 years ago. Since then, the languages on both sides have changed beyond recognition. No relationship could possibly be recognised.

As mentioned in chapter 7, many Australian languages have retroflex consonants, with the tongue turned back against the hard palate. They sound like languages from India which make much use of retroflex sounds. Does this similarity of pronunciation mean that languages of India are related to those of Australia? No, absolutely not.

So far in this book, Australian languages have been discussed as they once were. But that happy state was impinged upon by the arrival of intruders from Europe. To this we now turn our attention.

12

In recent times

Language communities do not exist in isolation. There is always contact—of varying kinds—with nearby peoples. This can include trade of foods and artefacts, meetings for sports or dance and song, excursions for study or just for vacation, and inter-group marriage. Many people in a community will acquire some knowledge of neighbouring languages, and a number will be fluent in them. Inevitably, linguistic features migrate as a consequence of social intermingling.

The main focus of borrowing (as it is called) is nouns. If some artefact or ceremony or foodstuff is adopted from another community, it is likely to bring its name with it. Verbs are borrowed rather less often, and grammatical affixes and suchlike scarcely at all. A language may copy a grammatical pattern from another language (say, a new way of marking possession) but is likely to express it using some of its existing forms.

Each language is thus a blend of genetic inheritance from the proto-language, and things borrowed from adjacent languages with which it is now in contact (these may or may not be genetic relatives). As a rule these two elements can be fairly well distinguished. The basic grammar and the most common words (especially verbs) are indicators of genetic affiliation. English, for instance, has a considerable number of lexical borrowings from French, but it is clearly a Germanic tongue on the basis of Germanic grammar and the most commonly occurring verbs. For example, all the irregular verbs (*show/showed/shown*, *give/gave/given*, and around 150 more) are Germanic. Borrowings from French and other languages have a lower frequency of use, and show entirely regular inflection (for instance, *please/pleased/pleased*).

The nature of the interaction between two nations is reflected in the words that are borrowed. For example, the Romans established a wine trade with Germanic speakers. This led to borrowings from Latin into Old English (around the end of the first millennium) such as *win* 'wine', and *flasce* 'a container for wine' (related to modern-day *flask*).

word in English	borrowing into Dyirbal, with gender marker
gown	bala gawun 'lady's dress'
money	bayi mani 'money'
sugar	balam juga 'sugar'
melon	balam milan 'water melon'
orange	balam ngarriñji 'orange'
iron	bala ngayan 'any iron artefact'
musket	bala marrgin 'any gun'
bullet	bala bulin 'bullet'

The type of contact between speakers of Dyirbal and the English people who intruded onto their land in the late nineteenth century is illustrated by the selection of borrowings in the box: an item of clothing, the new phenomenon of money, novel foods, the first metal encountered, and firearms.

Each borrowing is assigned to one of the four genders, which were described in chapter 9. 'Sugar', 'melon', and 'orange' are in the 'edible plant food' gender shown by *balam*, while 'gown', 'iron', 'musket', and 'bullet' are in the 'residue' class, shown by *bala*. 'Money' takes gender marker *bayi*, like human males, non-human animates, thunderstorm, and boomerang; no explanation was forthcoming for this. In some instances the era in which a word was borrowed is evident. The basic female garment was called a *gown* in the 1880s, a *frock* in the 1930s, and today *dress* would be preferred.

When a word is borrowed into another language, its pronunciation must be adapted to the patterns of the new language. Dyirbal has just three vowels (*i, a, u*) and each word must have at least two syllables. Thus *gown* becomes *gawun*. There is no *s* sound—the initial *s* in *sugar* is rendered by *j* in *juga* (this *j* is like *d* and *y* pronounced together) and the medial *s* in *musket* becomes a rolled *rr* in *marrgin*. A word in Dyirbal cannot end in *t* or *d*, so the final *t* in *musket* and *bullet* are replaced by *n* in *marrgin* and *bulin*. Final *ñj* is also not permitted so *i* is added at the end of *ngarriñji* 'orange'.

A word in Dyirbal cannot begin with a vowel; thus, for the borrowings based on *iron* and *orange*, an initial consonant must be added. And the one chosen is *ng* (phonetic [ŋ]), the sound which comes at the end of words in English (such as *ring* and *bang*) but not at the beginning of words. We get *ngayan* 'iron' and *ngarriñji* 'orange'. (The importance of being able to pronounce *ng* at the beginning of a word was illustrated by the anecdote with which chapter 7 began.)

Chapter 6 described how, for every word in the everyday speech style (Guwal) of Dyirbal, there is a corresponding word in the avoidance or 'mother-in-law' speech style (Jalnguy), and also how a single word in Jalnguy will relate to a set of related words in Guwal.

We have seen that English words are directly borrowed into Guwal with their forms being adjusted as necessary. But there are no borrowings into Jalnguy. What happens is that Jalnguy extends the scope of an existing word to also cover a borrowing. *Warruñ* is the Jalnguy correspondent for Guwal noun *waguy* 'sand', and it was also used for *juga* 'sugar' because of the similar consistency (made up of fine particles). Jalnguy *jujamu* corresponds to *bana* 'water' in Guwal and was extended to also cover *milan* 'watermelon', which (as shown by its name in English) does consist mostly of water.

Wouldn't this 'double naming' lead to confusion when speaking in Jalnguy style? Not at all. Disambiguation is achieved by gender markers:

	GUWAL	JALNGUY
'sand'	bala waguy	bala warruñ
'sugar'	balam juga	balam warruñ
'water'	balan bana	balan jujamu
'watermelon'	balam milan	balam jujamu

Both 'sugar' and 'watermelon' are in the 'edible plant food' gender, shown by *balam*, while 'water', being a 'drinkable liquid', takes *balan*, and 'sand' is in the 'residue' gender, with *bala*.

When two languages come into contact, borrowings go in both directions. Once speakers of English entered Australia they needed names for the local animals, birds, artefacts, and suchlike. The first visitors with enquiring minds were James Cook and Joseph Banks, who—during their short stay in 1770—had cordial relations with the local people around what is now called Cooktown. There were several varieties of large macropods in that country, each being accorded a distinct name in the local language, Guugu Yimidhirr. These included:

bibal	small scrub kangaroo
gangurru	large black or grey kangaroo
nharrgali	large red kangaroo
wudul	whip-tail kangaroo
dhulmbanu	wallaroo

Cook was particularly taken with a type of animal 'of a light mouse Colour and the full size of a Grey Hound, and shaped in every respect like one, with a long tail, which it carried like a Grey Hound; in short I should have taken it for a wild dog but for its walking or running, in which it jump'd like a Hare or Deer.' He elicited *kangaroo* or *kanguru* and incorrectly imagined that this name covered all types of kangaroo, whereas in fact it applies to only one species, the large black or grey animal. The word in Guugu Yimidhirr has a single consonant *ng* (phonetic [ŋ]) between the first and second vowels but, seeing the written form *kangaroo*, English speakers tend to insert a *g* after the *ng*, saying /kaŋgaru/ rather than /kaŋaru/. (As mentioned in chapter 7, the initial consonant can be pronounced as *k* or as *g*, and written in either way.)

There has been considerable confusion about the authenticity of this name. In 1820 Captain Phillip P. King visited the Endeavour

River, and took down a vocabulary that agreed with Cook's in every word except one. Instead of *kangooroo* he was given a word transcribed as 'min-ār', 'mee-nuah', or 'mēn-ū-āh'. Some people thought that Cook and Banks had made a mistake and there was even the preposterous suggestion that when asked the name of the animal a Guugu Yimidhirr person had said 'I don't understand' or 'I don't know', this being the true meaning of the word *kangaroo*.

In the early 1970s, linguist John Haviland undertook an intensive study of Guugu Yimidhirr and again recorded /*kaɲurru*/ (or /*gaɲurru*/). He pointed out that the word recorded in 1820 must have been the general term *minha* 'edible animal'. King probably pointed at several species of kangaroo other than the large black variety, and the Guugu Yimidhirr might not have connected his pronunciation /kaŋ-gəru/ with their word /kaɲurru/ or /gaɲuru/.

Cook was on shore for just a short time, while repairing his damaged vessel. Then, in 1788, there came to Sydney Cove people who intended to stay for ever. Joseph Banks had provided his manuscript vocabulary of the 'New Holland language', without specifying in what part of the continent it had been recorded. Governor Arthur Phillip mistakenly thought that it must have been taken down near Sydney (or perhaps that a single language was spoken over the whole continent). Members of the First Fleet employed the word *kangaroo* in talking to the local people, and must have used it in connection with a variety of marsupials. The Sydney people thought they were being taught the English word for 'edible animal'; when cattle were unloaded the local folk enquired whether they were *kangaroo*.

In his account of the fauna around Sydney, Captain Watkin Tench remarked that 'the bird which principally claims attention is a species of ostrich, approaching nearer to the emu of South

America than any other we know of'. That became its name in English—*emu* (said to be from Portuguese), rather than *marayang*, the name in the original language of the Sydney region.

However, most new phenomena did receive English names based on what they were called in the original language of Sydney. *Boomerang* was mentioned in chapter 4. Also *dingo*, *wombat*, *wallaby*, *waratah*, *woomera*, *corroboree*, and several dozen more. They included *koala*, about which a myth has been spun.

language	spoken around	'koala'
YAGARRA	Brisbane	marrangpi
BANDJALANG	Clarence River	burbi
GUMBAYNGGIRR	Coffs Harbour	dunggirr
DHARUK	Sydney	kula, kulawañ
WUYWURRUNG	Melbourne	gurrburra

This sedate, mainly nocturnal, tree-dwelling marsupial lives in sclerophyll forests and woodlands not far from the east and southeast coasts; the box provides names in five languages. In the Sydney language it was called *kula* or *kulawañ*, and the shorter form was soon adopted as the name in English; it was at first spelled *coola* or *koola* or *koolah*. Then a new spelling *koala* came into use, probably due to scribal error from *koola*. Towards the end of the nineteenth century both names—*koola* and *koala*—were in use, but *koola* gradually dropped out, being replaced by (the basically erroneous) *koala*.

Then the myth. On a visit to virtually any zoo in Australia, you will be told that the name *koala* means 'doesn't drink' in 'the Aboriginal language'. This is utterly without foundation. The original designation was *koola*, only at Sydney, and it is just a name, with no other meaning. (Most animal names are just that. For instance, *dog* doesn't mean 'barks' or *turtle* 'moves slowly'.) But the myth is firmly engrained, and it is cute, making it hard to expunge.

Several hundred words from dozens of the original languages have been taken into English. *Budgerigar* comes from Gamilaraay (Kamilaroi) in northern New South Wales, *kookaburra* from Wiradjuri, a little further south, and so on. Many are terms for plants and animals found only in limited regions. Just a few have found wide currency; for example, *kangaroo, boomerang, koala, dingo,* and *wombat* feature in dictionaries of Dutch, French, German, Portuguese and Russian, slightly adjusted into a form appropriate for the borrowing language. Hindi has *bumeraang* and *kangeroo*, while Japanese includes *bumeran* and *kangaru*.

Mandarin Chinese generally prefers not to borrow words from other languages, instead creating descriptions from its own resources. For example:

hui	fei	biao		dai	shu
return	fly	dart		bag	mouse
'boomerang'				**'kangaroo'**	

A boomerang is aptly described as 'a flying dart which returns' while a kangaroo is 'a (rather large) mouse with a bag (that is, the pouch in which the joey matures)'.

A full account of the 430 words adopted into English from the original languages is in *Australian Aboriginal Words in English: Their origin and meaning*, by Dixon et al. (1990, 2nd edition 2006),

For each borrowing, information is given on date of first use, the language it was taken from, and its original form and meaning.

Language contact extends beyond names. Each society has its own social institutions, conventions, and concepts, which may seem peculiar to outsiders. The original people of Australia operated with intricate sets of obligations, determined by kinship links. The British invaders were not aware of these, nor would most of them want to know. But—on the other side of the fence—the white people's practices could not be ignored. These were simply imposed on the original inhabitants.

For instance, the idea of 'work'. The original Australians did what was necessary, as required. One might assist another in a tricky task. But there was no concept of some activities being 'work' and others not. Nor of 'stopping work', nor of 'one person working for another'. All of this had to be learnt.

In order to survive, the original communities needed to adjust to the white people's ways, which came to be enforced across the continent. In most languages, borrowings are confined to nouns. English *work* or *working* became *warrgang* in Gumbaynggirr, *waarka* or *waaka* in different dialects of the Western Desert language, and *wagi* in Dyirbal. A verbalising suffix is then added: in Dyirbal we get verb *wagi-bin* 'work, be working'. However, a few languages extend the meaning of an existing word (rather similar to what happens in Mandarin Chinese). Nyawaygi—spoken just south of Ingham, in North Queensland—has adjective *magal* 'tired' and the concept of work is rendered by a verb derived from this; *magul-i* is 'work, be working' (it is literally 'become tired').

Every human community, right across the globe, operates with a concept of 'possession' but the scope of this varies immensely.

Different views of 'possession'—between the original inhabitants of Australia and the white-skinned invaders—were the major factor precipitating conflict and rampant murder.

An original Australian would own artefacts and the dwelling they had built. The idea of possession could be extended to a pet dog, but that was all. Most importantly, there was absolutely no concept of ownership over land. Each nation had an *association* with a particular place, which they had a strict responsibility to take care of and maintain. One might say that it was the people who belonged to the land, rather than vice versa. And, just as the people looked after the land, so the land provided for them, with roots to dig, fruits to pick, fish to catch, and animals to hunt.

Then came the British, with totally different ideas. They claimed—or were allocated by the government—title over a tract of land. Fences were erected, bush cleared, sheep and cows introduced. All this became their possession. The original people had retreated but were still there, requiring sustenance. Where kangaroos and emus had once roamed, there was now livestock. Surely a difference only of type. So they speared a cow.

But this cow was a possession of the 'settler'. Killing a cow was a crime and the miscreants must be taught a lesson. So the white men jumped on their horses, took up guns, galloped until they found a 'native camp' and slaughtered everyone there. The actual cow-killers might not have been from that particular camp but no matter, the intention was to 'teach the blacks a lesson'. To let them know that these animals—on land considered by the settler to be owned by him—were his property, and not open game like the kangaroos they had replaced. It was a question of possession.

Then came retribution. A homestead might be attacked and some of the occupants speared. Then a whole community, a dozen or more people, would be shot in counter-retribution. Only one side could win; as an elderly Dyirbal friend explained it to me, 'Spears were no match for guns. If we'd had guns it would have been a different story.'

However, eliminating resistance met obstacles. The original inhabitants knew the terrain to which they belonged and could be hard to root out. So an ingenious and lethal tactic was introduced. It is a natural trait of humankind to fear strangers, and wish to destroy them. A Native Police (or Black Police) Force was established, each unit commanded by a ruthless white officer and made up of half-a-dozen 'natives' from a faraway place, men who would have no compunction against slaying people of an alien nation. Whenever a settler reported that there was predation on his flocks, troopers from the Native Police would descend to track down the perpetrators. There was a special vocabulary used in official reports: 'All the offending natives were dispersed' simply meant that there were none left alive.

A.J. Vogan, in his book *The Black Police: A story of modern Australia*, wrote:

> A young 'sub', new in the force . . . used the word 'killed' in place of the official 'dispersed' in speaking of the unfortunate natives left hors de combat on the field. The report was returned to him for correction in company with a severe reprimand for his careless wording of the same. The 'sub', being rather a wag in his own way . . . corrected his report so that the faulty portion now read as follows: 'We successfully surrounded the said party of aborigines and dispersed fifteen, the remainder, some half dozen, succeeded in escaping.'

Matters had progressed so that, by about 1900, there was no longer need for the Native Police. Quite a number of the original people were living—and often working as servants—on the fringes of the white community. However, fear has not gone away. Many languages have an 'aversive' suffix which can be added to nouns, meaning 'for fear of'. One might hear 'Don't sit too close to the fire, flying sparks-AVERSIVE (for fear of flying sparks).' The most common noun to which the aversive ending is attached is 'policeman'. A car is heard coming down the track, and the warning goes out 'Hide policeman-AVERSIVE (for fear of the policeman)!'

Indeed the social relationships between cops and the original inhabitants are revealed by names for 'policeman'. For some languages it is a simple borrowing: in Gumbaynggirr *gañjibal*, from *constable*, and in Dyirbal *bulijiman*, from *policeman* (often shortened to *buliman*). But in others an officer of the law is accorded a descriptive label:

- In Walmatjari, from the Fitzroy River in Western Australia, the word for 'policeman' is *limpa* 'a fly which hovers and suddenly dives in to bite'.
- In Kalkatungu, spoken between Cloncurry and Mount Isa, it is *ganimay-ñjirr* 'he who ties people up'.
- In Djapu, from Arnhem Land, it is *dhapthap*, from the verb 'clench or grip', referring to the action of handcuffs.
- Anthropologist A.P. Elkin remarked: 'The Broome district words for policeman tell their own story: in Karadjeri he is called *weder*, fierce, severe-looking; in Yauor, *lendo*, sour, salty; and in Djaru *yawadaro wainowadji*, the chaining horseman.'

In 1986, the Queensland Museum moved into a grand new building with one exhibit presenting a panorama of Dyirbal traditional life—cutting a shield from a tree flange, fishing with butterfly nets, and so on. The museum brought about twenty

Dyirbal people down to Brisbane in a bus to celebrate the opening. As we were driving through the city, there was a cry 'Stop the bus!' A policeman was on point duty, directing traffic, and the people wanted to take a photo of what they considered to be a remarkable sight. It was the first time they had ever seen a policeman doing something which they regarded as useful.

The years since 1788 have provided a rough passage for the original peoples of Australia, and for their wondrous languages. Just a few continue to be actively used. Others were pushed into abeyance a few generations back; however, in quite a few instances there are developing programs to revive them. The final chapter briefly surveys some of the recent developments.

13

The languages today

Some years back, my office at the Australian National University was invaded by a TV news crew. Arc light shimmering, microphone probing. First question:

'Do you think that white people bear some responsibility for the loss of Aboriginal language and culture?'

'Yes, of course.'

'How, then?'

'By coming here in the first place.'

I don't believe that interview made it to the screen. The plain truth is often not welcome; there is preference for milder, friendlier statements which will not offend.

Each year there is a public holiday on 26 January, 'Australia Day', to commemorate the landing in 1788 of 750 convicts (sent to Australia because America had declared independence and would no longer accept them) together with 213 marines to keep order. Some members of the First Nations say that it should be renamed 'Invasion Day'; others suggest 'Day of Mourning'.

Just what is the message here? That the English—and French and Dutch and so on—should have stayed away? So that the original people of Australia could remain in their pristine state? (Even until today?) No clothing, no permanent houses or furniture, no cabbage, carrot or cauliflower, no sugar or salt, no beef or chicken or lamb, no reading or writing, no tobacco or alcohol. More recently, no electricity, radio, films, TV, or mobile phones. Might it truly have been possible for the Indigenous people to remain isolated from the rest of the world? To have repelled all invaders and sent them packing?

There is an example of this kind. North Sentinel Island, the westernmost member of the Andaman archipelago in the Bay of Bengal, is about the size of Manhattan, thickly wooded, and surrounded with submerged coral reefs. The first European to notice the island was John Ritchie, a surveyor on the East India Company hydrographic survey vessel *The Diligent*. This was in 1771, the year after Cook's journey up the east coast of Australia. Ritchie noticed lights on shore, showing that North Sentinel was inhabited. But to this day we don't know the size of the population; estimates vary from several score to a few hundred.

The North Sentinelese are immensely hostile and any attempt to land is resisted with a hail of arrows. In 1880 there was an armed British expedition but the people simply retreated into the jungle until the outsiders had departed. Smaller groups of visitors are killed. In 2006 two men whose fishing boat drifted near shore were riddled with arrows. Today, the Indian government has declared an exclusion zone around the island, insisting that the people be left alone. It is feared that, if forcibly contacted, they would fall prey to diseases against which they have no immunity. In November 2018 an American 'missionary' was able to sneak ashore, only to be killed and buried on the beach.

Is that what people who declare a 'Day of Mourning' would like to have happened? But Australia could not have remained aloof from the world at large in the way that North Sentinel Island has. It is too big, in too strategic a position, too suitable for agriculture and livestock, too replete with precious and other metals. Invasion was inevitable.

What can be questioned is the manner in which the invasion was conducted. Basically, this relates to the attitudes of the two parties involved: the original inhabitants on the one side, and the intruders on the other.

Traders from the Macassan Islands had been making annual visits to a few places on the central north coast since the late 1600s but, apart from this, the original inhabitants of Australia had had no contact with outsiders. Two factors now come into play. First, Australian religion focused on the spirits of ancestors. And secondly, after someone dies their black skin turns a lighter colour. The white-skinned visitors were not at first perceived as a threat; on the contrary, they were believed to be the returned spirits of the people's ancestors. 'By the time we found out this was not so,' I was told, 'it was a bit late, the Englishmen had taken advantage of our goodwill.'

In the early days of contact, from the 1860s, Dyirbal people referred to a white man as *guwuy* 'spirit of a dead man' and a white woman as *guynggan* 'spirit of a dead woman'. Later, after realisation that the intruders were not returned relatives but unsympathetic outsiders, these labels were replaced by borrowings: *waybala* 'white man', from *white fellow*, and *mijiji* 'white woman', from *missus*. But the association was still there in the avoidance or 'mother-in-law' style, Jalnguy:

	GUWAL	JALNGUY
'spirit of a dead man'	bayi guwuy	bayi gumirriñ
'white man'	bayi waybala	
'spirit of a dead woman'	balan guynggan	balan yurrigan
'white woman'	balan mijiji	

The North Sentinelese would have had contact with marauders from India or Burma for many centuries before 1771, and—up until today—recognise the menace which all outsiders pose for their way of life. The original people of Australia—spread sparsely across an island continent—had little time to come to this realisation.

That is one side of the contact situation. What now of the other side, the attitude of white people in the First Fleet, and their successors who soon spread out to appropriate every economically attractive portion of the continent? First of all, Dampier's uninformed summation still resounded: 'the miserablest people in the world'. (If it had an effect when told to me, an English schoolboy, in the 1940s, it would surely have had stronger force at Sydney Cove a century and a half earlier.)

Sure, the British government had instructed the colonists that the rights of the original inhabitants should be respected, but such stipulations were conveniently ditched overboard during the voyage out. After all, the invaders could see for themselves: these people had no clothes, no settled place of habitation, no chiefs or social order, they did not practise agriculture, they spoke a language which was—on no evidence—supposed to have few words and no grammar, and they did not worship a single supreme being. It became accepted that it was the responsibility of the English to take over this land of opportunity. And the original peoples? Well, they could stick around if they didn't get in the way. However, they frequently did.

Depopulation engendered by the invaders began before any shot was fired in anger. Introduced diseases soon commenced their lethal effects: smallpox, tuberculosis, syphilis, and influenza. Within two years of the first settlement, more than half the population around Sydney had died from smallpox, and the virus then spread across much of the continent. Three further epidemics of smallpox are reported in the nineteenth century. By the time white people reached some new region, the germs would have preceded them. Local communities had been so reduced—in numbers and in spirit—that their resistance was more muted than it would otherwise have been.

Then came the settlers' massacres of anyone who threatened their livelihood, assisted by the Native Police. Around 1900, attitudes changed. Many of the original people who still survived were rounded up, taken from their traditional lands (with which they had a natal association), and dispatched to government reserves and church missions, which in certain aspects resembled prisons. A few people who were useful to the newly dominant race were allowed to remain free, the women generally working as house-maids and the men as farm labourers.

How did the usurped people's languages survive among such upheavals? Badly. Unfamiliar tongues were regarded by the whites as subversive. Station owners often forbade stockmen to speak in anything but English; the owner must be able to understand everything that was said, in case a plot was being hatched against him (which might well be the case). In missions and government reserves, children were separated into boys' and girls' dormitories.

No contact between the sexes and not much with parents, who they might be allowed to see for a couple of hours each Saturday. Little chance of the cultural heritage being passed on. And speaking in the original languages was absolutely forbidden, any transgressor receiving corporal punishment. The children of those of the original people who lived in the community at large were for many years not welcomed in all-white schools. When eventually they were admitted, any talking in the native language attracted whacks of the cane.

The nomenclature employed is of interest. New Holland was the first name for the continent, and the original inhabitants were the New Hollanders. When, in the 1810s, the place was re-named Australia, the New Hollanders became the Australians. But not for long. By the 1820s white people born in Australia usurped the designation Australians, and the people they were displacing had to be referred to as Aboriginal Australians (or, using an adjective as a noun, Aboriginals) or just Aborigines.

The number of First Nations people fell rapidly in the southeast, where white settlement was concentrated. Besides disease and murder it seems that the original inhabitants had little wish to beget children into the alien new world. However, quite a few white men took an Aboriginal partner and, as the number of so-called 'full-bloods' (a term used around the world at that time) diminished, so there were many 'half-castes' (as people of blended heritage were then called). All of these people were denied the status of citizens in their own land. When the six colonies combined, in 1901, to form a single nation, section 127 of the Constitution read: 'In reckoning the numbers of the people of the Commonwealth, or of a State or other part of the Commonwealth, aboriginal natives shall not be counted.'

More than this, 'Aborigines', including half-castes, were not even regarded as people. In Queensland, for example, they were not permitted to partake of alcohol, and they could not even access their own savings accounts. The local policeman held each Aborigine's bank book so that deposits and withdrawals went through him. 'Here's ten pounds for you, Johnny', he might say, at the same time slipping five pounds into his own pocket. In one western Queensland town, the policeman drove around in a smart new car paid for by such misappropriations. 'There goes our car,' the local Aborigines bewailed.

Public feeling did shift. There was a national referendum in 1967 and—greatly to the prime minister's surprise—91 per cent voted to remove section 127 from the Constitution. During the 1970s there was an upsurge of interest in the original peoples. Enrolments in Aboriginal Studies courses surged for a while (and then declined).

The distinction between full-blood and 'part-blood' (for a time, considered a more acceptable term than half-caste) came to be considered inappropriate. Everyone who had one of the original inhabitants in their family tree was simply just an 'Aborigine'. 'Land rights' had been granted to people in the north who had retained much of their own culture and language; then people in the south made similar but sometimes unsubstantiable claims. Public sympathy waned. There was another referendum in 1999, not to change the Constitution but simply to add a preamble which included: 'honouring Aborigines and Torres Strait Islanders, the nation's first people, for their deep kinship with their lands and for their ancient and continuing cultures which enrich the life of our country'. This was rejected, with only 39 per cent saying 'yes'; it would probably have been adopted 25 years earlier.

'Aborigine' had always been an unfortunate term (outside the Australian context it has a derogatory overtone) and, as the 21st century loomed, this was relegated to history (rather like 'Negro' in the US), being replaced by 'Indigenous People'. The new term covers everyone who is in any way descended from the original inhabitants, opts to identify themself in this way, and is accepted as a member of an Indigenous community. Around 2010, the term 'Nation' came into use, these making up the 'First Nations'.

How have the original languages survived through all of this? Recall that there were originally about 250 of them, each as different from the others as French and Hungarian. Sadly, less than twenty are still actively used in everyday discourse. A few are remembered by a handful of elderly speakers. The remainder have fallen out of use. For some of these the written records are slight—just a couple of short word lists, badly transcribed. But, during the nineteenth century, missionaries and amateur scholars provided quite detailed vocabularies and grammars for a number of languages and today these form the basis for ambitious programs of language revival.

Today, many Indigenous People speak a dialect of English. The language has many dialects, all mutually intelligible. People in Glasgow use a variety of the same language as those in New York and Auckland. There are of course some differences between dialects, but these are minor and do not affect the speakers' ability to understand each other. The English spoken by most Indigenous

Australians is another dialect, differing from the others in small but interesting ways. This is illustrated by the four sample sentences:

	STANDARD DIALECT	INDIGENOUS DIALECT
1	He's got a dog	Ee got one dog
2	He's got two dogs	Ee got two dog
3	He's got three dogs	Ee got three dog
4	He's got dogs	Ee got plenty dog

Let us examine the differences. The Indigenous dialect drops initial *h*, so that *he* becomes *ee* (quite a lot of other dialects do the same thing). The verb phrase *has got* is reduced by *'s got* in the Standard dialect, and further reduced to just *got* in the Indigenous one. For sentence 1, the Indigenous dialect has *one* corresponding to *a* (in fact, this indefinite article developed from number word 'one' in an earlier stage of English). None of these affect meaning. More significant is that the plural ending -*s* has been lost from the Indigenous variety. This doesn't matter for sentences 2 and 3 since they include number words *two* and *three* (that is, the -*s* suffix on *dog* is redundant here). In sentence 4, plural is marked by adjective *plenty* in the right-hand column. This is similar in form to *He's got plenty of dogs* in the Standard dialect, but here *plenty of dogs* indicates a goodly number, or an ample number, whereas in the Indigenous dialect *plenty* is just a marker of plural.

There is one way in which the Indigenous variety is superior. In this dialect, the noun *dog* carries no assumption of number. The sentence *Ee got dog* indicates that he has some number of dogs— it could be one or more than one. In contrast, for the Standard dialect *dog* always indicates singular and *dogs* plural number. To translate the Indigenous sentence *Ee got dog* into Standard English one would need to say: *He's got one or more dogs*, or *He's got some number of dogs*. The Indigenous dialect can be usefully vague in this respect, whereas the Standard one must be specific.

It needs to be stressed that the Indigenous variety is not just 'bad English', as is sometimes suggested. It is simply a different dialect, with its own set of coherent structural principles, just like every other dialect.

Across the northern part of the continent, many Indigenous people speak a dialect of Creole (also spelled Kriol). This has most of its lexical words (and some grammatical forms) based on English, but they are adapted to the prevalent sound patterns of the original languages. Its grammatical contrasts and structures are similar to those of the local languages. Creole is a distinct language, not mutually intelligible either with English or with any of the original languages (it thus differs from Indigenous varieties of English).

In the area where Creole is now used, the original languages have complex word structures, including 'bound pronouns' as affixes to a verbal element; this was illustrated for Nyigina in chapter 8. Another example comes from Walmatjari, spoken around the Fitzroy River in Western Australia:

(1) | Debi-karti | ma-rna | yan-i |
|---|---|---|
| Derby-TO | DECLARATIVE-1sg | go-PAST |

I went to Derby

Here the verb *yan-* 'go' takes past tense suffix *-i*. It is preceded by modal root *ma-*, showing that the sentence is a statement (for a question, *ma-* would be replaced by *nga-*, and for a command

there would be no modal root at all). To *ma-* is suffixed bound
pronoun *-rna*, indicating that the subject of the sentence is 1st
person singular, 'I'. And suffix *-karti* onto place name *Debi* 'Derby'
corresponds to preposition *to* in English.

Nowadays, younger members of the Walmatjari nation use the
local variety of Creole in which this sentence would come out as:

(2)	Ai	bin	go	la	Debi
	1sg	PAST	go	TO	Derby

I went to Derby

Words in Creole have a simpler structure than those in Walmatjari.
The 1st person singular subject pronoun is here a separate word *ai*
(based on English *I*). Past tense is shown by a separate word *bin*,
before the verb. To indicate 'to', Creole uses a preposition *la* (just like
English *to*), in contrast to Walmatjari which employs suffix *-karti*.

Sentence (2) is straightforward. But many aspects of Creole are
less obvious and far more complex, reflecting recurrent features
of the original languages. This grammatical congruence can be
illustrated by comparing pronoun systems. The bound pronouns in
Walmatjari can be augmented by free-form pronouns, the complete
system of these being:

	SINGULAR	DUAL	PLURAL
1st person inclusive	ngaju	ngali-jarra	ngali-mpa
1st person exclusive		nga-jarra	ngani-mpa
2nd person	ñuntu	ñurra-jarra	ñurra-warnti
3rd person	ñantu	ñantu-jarra	ñantu-warnti

Subject pronouns in the local Fitzroy Valley variety of Creole show exactly the same contrasts, with a singular/dual/plural number system, and a distinction between inclusive (including 'you') and exclusive (not including 'you') for 1st person dual and plural. Below the forms in Creole, it is instructive to indicate—in parentheses— the forms on which they are based (using English orthography).

Subject pronouns in the Fitzroy Valley dialect of Creole:

	SINGULAR	DUAL	PLURAL
1st person inclusive		minyu (*me-n-you*)	wilat (*we-lot*)
1st person exclusive	ai (*i*)	midupela (*me-two-fellow*)	mipela (*me-fellow*)
2nd person	yu (*you*)	yundupela (*you-two-fellow*)	yupela (*you-fellow*)
3rd person	i (*he*)	dupela (*two-fellow*)	dei (*they*)

Sentence (2) was simple and fairly easily understandable. The character of Creole is more fully illustrated by:

(3)	Mipela	bin	tjak-in-abat		najing
	1pl(exclusive)	PAST	throw-CONTINUOUS-REPEATED		in.vain

We all (not including you) kept on casting (our fishing lines) for a long time, but it was all in vain (that is, we caught nothing)

The verb in (3) takes two suffixes: continuous -*in*, and repeated action -*abat*. Note that verb *tjak*- 'throw' is based on English *chuck*, and adverb *najing* 'in vain' comes from *nothing*. Nevertheless, a speaker of English could not get a full understanding of (3). Despite varied similarities to its progenitors, Creole is a separate language, which has to be learnt.

Languages sometimes die gradually, each generation knowing a little less than the previous one. Other times the demise can be abrupt—one generation has fluent competence but their children learn little. In the Australian context, such 'sudden death' has been common. When children were separated from parents, placed in dormitories and punished if heard speaking anything but English, there was little opportunity for the chain of language inheritance to be maintained. For those living within mainstream society, parents—although themselves fully competent in a traditional tongue—might choose to speak to their children only in English, as a way of helping them succeed in the white man's world. Or the children themselves may make this choice, eschewing traditional ways as 'old-fashioned'.

Languages die quickest in places which the invader exploits the most—whether for rearing livestock, or digging out gold, or growing sugar cane, or whatever. The Yidiñ language was spoken just south of the present city of Cairns (founded in 1876). There was disease, murder, dormitories, the usual story. In the 1970s and 1980s the last six fluent speakers (born between about 1890 and 1920) were delighted to tell me stories, explain place names, and list and illustrate every word that could be remembered. It was as if they had been waiting for someone like me to come along, 'to get it all down on paper and on tape' before it was too late. Almost nothing of this ancient language had been passed on to the next generations.

However, there is today a new sense of ethnic awareness and pride among the Yidiñji nation (and the neighbouring Gungañji nation, which spoke another dialect of the same language). A school syllabus has been developed, based on what their grandparents had taught me. I sent cassettes and CDs of stories recorded more than forty years before. The language had been in abeyance but it now is re-awakening.

Speakers of Dyirbal, the next language to the south, were perhaps fortunate in that their territory was less sought after. One group continued a traditional life-style, in the jungle around the headwaters of the Tully River, until the 1940s. Whereas Yidiñ passed out of use between one generation and the next, Dyirbal lingered a while. There were several score fluent speakers when I began work in the 1960s, but everyone in the community also knew some English. Twenty years later, all the fluent speakers were middle-aged or older, and the local variety of Aboriginal English had become the main means of communication.

However, there was a group of young people, then aged in their twenties, who spoke a modified form of Dyirbal among themselves. They used a smaller vocabulary than their parents, and a simplified grammar. The intriguing system of four genders in traditional Dyirbal was described in chapter 9. Young speakers had lost the 'edible plant food' gender (previously shown by *balam*) and all the subtle principles for gender transfer. In fact, their three genders— shown by *bayi*, *balan*, and *bala*—corresponded quite closely to the English pronouns *he*, *she*, and *it*. In legend, 'sun' and 'moon' were wife and husband, being therefore *balan* (female human) and *bayi* (male human) respectively; both were now in the 'residue' class, shown by *bala*. 'Water', 'fire', and harmful plants, previously *balan*, were also now *bala*.

Traditional Dyirbal has the following suffixes on nouns: *-ngga* for 'at', *-gu* for 'to', and *-ngunu* for 'from'. Some young people tended to use *-ngga* for all three meanings (only the context of speaking might distinguish them). We can see how a sentence in the traditional language was rendered by young people:

ORIGINAL DYIRBAL	Ngaja	yanu	mija-ngunu
	I	go.PAST	house-FROM
I went from the house			
YOUNG PEOPLE'S DYIRBAL	Ngaja	yanu-n	mija-ngga

'Go' is the only irregular verb in Dyirbal, and its past tense form is *yanu*. Young people treated it as a regular verb and added past tense suffix *-n*. A further development is that some young people did not use any suffixes on nouns, substituting English prepositions, and also included English lexical items in their modified Dyirbal (such as *Bayi olman ñina-ñu on yugu* 'The <u>old</u> <u>man</u> sat <u>on</u> a log').

The last fluent speaker of traditional Dyirbal died in 2011. The 'young people' of the early 1980s do still, on occasion, speak their diminished variety, but they are now in their sixties. Later generations may know a few words but could not sustain a conversation. Thus has the language gradually faded away.

The languages which survive most strongly are found in the more remote regions, which have been little touched by the avarice of white men. Some have a healthy cadre of speakers but it is generally reported that the younger generation employs a more restricted linguistic repertoire, similar to the situation in Dyirbal.

The Pitjantjatjara dialect of the Western Desert language is described as 'alive and kicking', but the speech of teenagers is considerably modified from that of their elders. Free pronouns are now used much more than bound pronominal suffixes, several aspects of the grammar have been simplified, word order has become similar to that in English, and many English words are used. For instance, traditional Pitjantjatjara has *kurntili* for 'father's sisters' and *ngunyju* for 'mother' and 'mother's sisters'. Teenagers say *aanti* (from English *aunty*) for 'father's sisters' and 'mother's sisters', and *maama* (from English *mama*) for 'mother'.

Each of the original languages has an intricate grammar. Perhaps the most complex of all is found in Tiwi, spoken on Melville and Bathurst Islands (now known as the Tiwi Islands) just to the north of Darwin. When linguist Jennifer Lee worked on the islands, in the 1970s and 1980s, she found that people aged 55 and more were fluent in Traditional Tiwi (TT), but those in their teens and twenties could only just understand this, and themselves spoke a simplified variety, Modern Tiwi (MT).

Whereas TT has three demonstratives: 'this (near me)', 'this (near you)', and 'that (not near either of us)', MT only has two, having ceased to use the 'near you' form. The system of free form pronouns is also reduced:

	TT	MT		TT	MT
'I'	nglya	yiya	'she'	ñirra	thirra
'me and you'	muwa	—	'we'	ngawa	awa
'you (sg)'	nginja	yitha	'you (pl)'	nuwa	nuwa
'he'	ngarra	arra	'they'	wuta	wurra

MT has dropped the 'me and you' form *muwa*, and all of the other pronouns, except 'you (pl)' *nuwa*, have been phonetically reduced or changed.

The most notable feature of TT is the structure of the verb. Before the lexical root there are thirteen prefix positions and after it four possible suffixes. These indicate person and number of subject and object, tense, aspect, mood, and also whether something happened 'in the morning' or 'in the evening'. MT has fewer verbal affixes (but still more than most languages), with six prefix and three suffix positions. However, it uses bound pronominal prefixes less than does TT. We can compare:

TT	MT		
Yi-mini-pirni	Arra kilim yiya		
HE(SUBJECT).PAST-ME(OBJECT)-hit	HE	hit	ME
He hit me	**He hit me**		

In TT the sentence consists of just one word, with bound pronoun prefixes showing subject and object; also, the subject pronoun marks past tense (for non-past the initial prefix would have been *a-*). In contrast, MT employs free pronouns, with word order mirroring that of English. The TT verb root *-pirni-* 'hit' has been replaced by *kilim*; this comes from English *kill him*, but the meaning in MT is 'hit' rather than 'kill'.

MT does sometimes use pronominal prefixes, as in the following sentence. But note that there is still intrusion from English, with preposition *from*.

Yi-nuriyi	from	Putawani
HE(SUBJECT).PAST-come	FROM	Darwin

He came from Darwin

So, where are we now? The original inhabitants came to Australia 50,000 years (or more) ago, and until recently they spoke 250 distinct languages, as different from each other as Japanese and Chinese. The original cultures were markedly different from those of Europe. Material possessions were sufficient without being superfluous. Social organisation was highly developed; each person in a community was in a certain relationship to each other person, and this determined responsibilities and modes of behaviour. The character of the original languages reflected social norms and economic reality. There was a special speech-style, which must be used in the presence of a mother-in-law or son-in-law, to emphasise the avoidance relationship between them. For a nation living in the forest, replete with fruit and vegetables, a special grammatical gender was appropriate to classify these.

The white invaders came to exploit the land—whether by breeding livestock, growing sugar cane, or digging for gold. Anything in their way, such as the original inhabitants, would be either exploited or eliminated. Europeans came in haste and with a blinkered view, unaware of the richness of the age-old cultures they were seeking to displace. A measure of awareness did eventually emerge, but far too late. And members of the First Nations—those who survived—began at last to assert their birthright.

It is only in places which the invaders did not consider ripe for economic exploitation that a handful of the original languages are still in daily use. But outside influence intrudes; television, in English, is pervasive in even the more remote communities. As a consequence, younger people are adopting a reduced form of the traditional language.

There is, however, a brighter side to the picture. During recent years there have been ambitious efforts, across several states, to revive languages which ceased to be actively spoken some generations ago. Such programs are playing an important role in the reaffirmation of ethnic identity and sociocultural awareness. They merit a separate book, all to themselves.

Acknowledgements

Thanks are inadequate to those of the original inhabitants who transformed my life by accepting me into their communities, and entrusting me with preserving—on tape and on paper—their cultural and linguistic heritage. This book is dedicated to their memory—Chloe Grant, George Watson, Dick Moses, Mollie Raymond, Tilly Fuller, Bessie Jerry, John Tooth, Willie Seaton, Ida Henry, Spider Henry, Paddy Beeron, Andy Denham, George Davis, Tom Murray, Jimmy Murray, Daisy Denham, Tommy Springcart, and 50 more.

Tahnee Innes, Martin Duwell, Eelsha Dixon, Clare Allridge, Joshua Walker, and Brigitta Flick read through the whole volume and provided the most useful comments for improvement. A special debt of gratitude is due to Elizabeth Weiss, publisher at Allen & Unwin, whose cogent and constructive suggestions helped make it a better book.

I am grateful to Bai Junwei for how to say 'boomerang' and 'kangaroo' in Mandarin Chinese. And to Alan Dench for discussion concerning Dampier's second visit to New Holland, in 1699. Claire Smith, Peter Bellwood, and Sean Ulm advised about current opinions concerning how long ago the original inhabitants reached Australia.

Sources and notes

Foreword

Searching for Aboriginal Languages: Memoirs of a fieldworker by R.M.W. (Bob) Dixon is an account of work with the last speakers of languages in north-east Queensland. It was published in 1984 by the University of Queensland Press, reissued in 1989 by the University of Chicago Press, and then in 2011 by Cambridge University Press, from whom it is still available.

Chapter 1: Many distinct languages

- In Dixon et al. (1990: 2, 2006: 2), I first suggested that 'nation' was a more appropriate name than 'tribe'.
- Quote from 'Unpleasantness at Budleigh Court' from the short-story collection *Mr Mulliner Speaking* by P.G. Wodehouse (1929).
- Information on Dyirbal from Dixon (1972), on Bandjalang from Crowley (1978), and on Martuthunira from Dench (1995).
- The *Sydney Morning Herald* headline is from the issue of 15 December 1972.

Chapter 2: Each language has several dialects

- The mutual intelligibility of dialects of the Western Desert language was established by Hansen (1984).
- Quotation from page 609 of Churchill (1950).

Chapter 3: Language doing its job

- Information on black bean preparation and bark blanket making for Dyirbal is partly from my own fieldwork (including an account of blanket preparation from Bessie Jerry), and partly from a 1900 manuscript by Walter E. Roth 'On the natives of the (Lower) Tully River', and a 1898 one 'Some Ethnological Notes on the Atherton Blacks', both held in the Oxley Library, Brisbane.
- Information on named stages in an individual's life-cycle in Warlpiri is from Meggitt (1962: 233–6). His orthography is retained except that 'ŋ' is replaced by 'ng'.
- For 'initiation styles' see Dixon (2002: 91–2) and detailed references given there.
- A full account of Dyirbal songs is in Dixon and Koch (1996). The two songs quoted here are on pages 91–2 and 314.

Chapter 4: Nothing primitive here

- In 1623, 65 years before Dampier, Dutchman Jan Carstensz visited the west coast of the Cape York Peninsula in Queensland; his description of the people he encountered translates as 'the most wretched and poorest creatures that I have ever seen in my age or time' (Heeres 1899: 39; Mulvaney 1989: 13). However, this report did not achieve wide currency.
- Information on Bardi seasons and life-style from Bowern (2012: 27–39). Note that Bowern erroneously refers to the year of Dampier's visit as 1687 (it was actually 1688) and the month as March rather than January. She gives the date of publication for Dampier's *A New Voyage Round the World* as 1699; it was actually 1697. In addition, Bowern's survey of literature on the Bardi nation is incomplete; for example, she does not mention Elkin's (1935) detailed account of initiation rites.
- Information on Martuthunira from Dench (1995). The exact locations where Dampier came ashore on his 1699 visit to New Holland are not clear. He probably had contact with the Martuthunira and also the Ngarluma nation. Brown (1913) includes detailed ethnographic information relating to both groups.

- There are a number of editions of Cook's journal and I have consulted several. The long quotation is from Beaglehole (1955: 399).
- The Threlkeld quotation is from Gunson (1974, Vol. 1: 69). The prime source on boomerangs is Jones (1996); I have quoted from his pages 38–9 and 54. For an account, and map, of parts of Australia which lacked the boomerang see Dixon (2002: 13–14).

Chapter 5: Knowing who your relations are

- Indian English does supply the terms missing from Standard English. A spouse's sister-in-law (Sue in the diagram) is a 'co-sister-in-law', and a son or daughter's father-in-law (Tom in the other diagram) is a 'co-father-in-law'. See Dixon (2016: 151).
- Details of the Martuthunira kinship system are in Brown (1913: 175–90) and of the Bardi system in Elkin (1932: 310–17).
- The Dyirbal system is described in Dixon (1989), repeated in Dixon (2015: 61–83). One feature of the Dyirbal system which is particularly unusual (within the Australian context, and indeed generally) is that spouses are typically from alternate generations.
- Kinship systems, of the kind described here for Dyirbal, are only one part of the overall network of social organisation. In some communities everyone is divided between two 'moieties'; a spouse must come from the other moiety. Or there may be four 'sections'. For example, a man from section A will marry a woman from B, their son will be in C and will marry a woman from D, their son belonging to A; and so on. Or there may be eight 'sub-sections'. See the brief survey (with map) in Dixon (2002: 16–18) and further references therein.

Chapter 6: Who are you talking to?

- The avoidance style for Bunuba is described in Rumsey (2000: 123–8) and that for Guugu Yimidhirr in Haviland (1979a, 1979b, 1979c). The Jalnguy style for Dyirbal is dealt with in Dixon (2015: 85–111). Note that the everyday speech style is called Guwal in southern dialects of the language and Ngirrma in northern dialects.

- The procedure of asking for Jalnguy correspondents for Guwal verbs, and then—reversing things—Guwal correspondents for Jalnguy verbs was gone through with Chloe Grant and then, independently, with another intelligent and knowledgeable speaker, George Watson. The results were almost identical.

Chapter 7: Getting your tongue around it

- This chapter summarises some of the canonical features of phonological systems for the original languages of Australia. There are many variations on this theme; a full account can be found in Dixon (2002: 547–658). Just a few of the alternatives can be briefly mentioned here. Most of the c. 250 languages have two *r*-phonemes; however about twelve have just one, while around twenty have three. About sixty languages do have a contrast between two series of stops (this may involve voicing, fortition, gemination, aspiration, or a combination of these) or a contrast between a stop series and a fricative series. In a number of languages, some initial syllables have been dropped or truncated, leading to words commencing with a sequence of two consonants or a vowel. For example, in Mbabaram (spoken around Dimbulah, Petford, and Irvinebank in North Queensland), original *bamba* 'stomach' has become *mba*, and *waangal* 'boomerang' has become *angal*.
- Since many instances of orthographic *u* in English are pronounced as [ə], some orthographies for Australian languages prefer to write the /u/ phoneme as *oo*, in order to assist with the correct pronunciation.

Chapter 8: Putting the bits together

- Information on tenses in the language of West Torres Strait is based on Bani and Klokeid (1971), supplemented by information from speakers of the language.
- Data on pronouns in Guugu Yimidhirr from Haviland (1979a: 65); on pronouns in Lardil from Hale (1966); on bound pronouns in Nyigina from

Stokes (1982: 274, 239, 154, 170); on demonstratives in Bandjalang from Crowley (1978: 71); on demonstratives in Martuthunira from Dench (1995: 110).

- Description of demonstratives in the Yankunytjatjara dialect of the Western Desert language from Goddard (1983: 104–7); Glass and Hackett (1970: 50–2) provide an account of a very similar system in the Ngaanyatjara dialect of this language.
- Information on cases in Martuthunira is based on Dench (1995: 63–80).

Chapter 9: Remarkable genders

- Information on Indonesian from Sneddon (1996: 134–7, 184).
- A full account of classifiers in Yidiñ is in Dixon (2015: 44–60).
- The sample lists of snakes and trees are from pp. 156, 207 of the thesaurus-dictionary of Yidiñ in Dixon (1991).
- A full study of Dyirbal genders is in Dixon (2015: 21–43); the account given here is a considerably shortened version of it.
- There is a detailed survey of classifiers and genders across the original languages of Australia in Dixon (2002: 449–514).

Chapter 10: Oodles of words

- The account of *kapi*, and the quotation, are from Elkin (1937: 141). Discussion of *rlikan* 'elbow' in Yolngu from Morphy (1977: 87–91). Information on Yir-Yoront from Alpher (1991), on Guugu Yimidhirr from Haviland (1989).
- Evans and Wilkins (2000) have extensive discussion of the ear as the seat of intelligence in Australian languages.
- The discussion of *kunta* in Pintupi is from Myers (1976: 141–51).

Chapter 11: Are there any language links?

- The reconstruction of proto-Ngayarda phonology is in O'Grady (1966). For Jabugay-Yidiñ see Dixon (1977).

- There is more on the New Guinea/Australia land mass—and a map showing the considerable land bridge at 25,000 BP—in Dixon (2002: 7–12).
- There is no absolute agreement among archaeologists concerning the earliest date for human habitation in Australia. Almost everyone would accept a time-depth of 50,000 years, which is the figure quoted here. Some would embrace an earlier date of 60,000 or even 65,000 years, but this comes from a single excavation site. Others are at present dubious about this claim.
- The little information there is concerning the original languages of Tasmania is summarised in Crowley and Dixon (1981).
- Like every other discipline, linguistics has its crackpot fringe—people who transcend the limits of the accepted scientific methodology, and suggest unsubstantiable genetic linkages between distinct language families across Eurasia, across the Americas, across Africa, and across New Guinea. The crackest of pots have even put forward a (vague) 'proto-World' (spoken a mere 120,000 years ago).
- In order to convincingly prove that a group of languages are genetically related, a great deal of their putative proto-language needs to be reconstructed—at least four or five hundred lexemes, across all semantic domains (with the regular changes which produced the occurring forms in each modern language) plus a good deal of the grammar, including inflectional paradigms for nouns, pronouns, verbs, etc. None of this has been done—or could be done—to establish Pama-Nyungan as a genetic unit. (For a detailed discussion of the 'Pama-Nyungan idea' see Dixon 2002: 44–54.) Belief in Pama-Nyungan as a genetic family is something of an act of faith; and faith does not require reason.
- In recent years, a 'phylogenetic' method of language classification has been adapted from biology. This is an artefact, which manipulates a limited set of data in a playful way. It has no relevance with respect to the established discipline of comparative-historical linguistics.

Chapter 12: In recent times

- Information from King (1827, Vol. 2: 632–5) and from Haviland (1979a: 173; 1974).

- Note that early scribes provided varied spellings for 'emu' in the Dharuk language from the Sydney region; it may have been *marayang* or else *marawung*.
- Quotation from Tench (1979: 66).
- Quotations from Vogan (1891: 142) and Elkin (1937: 163).

Chapter 13: The languages today

- Accounts of smallpox epidemics are in Crosby (1986: 206).
- In 1964, The Australian Institute of Aboriginal Studies (AIAS) was established by the federal government. But the original inhabitants of the Torres Strait Islands pointed out that they were racially and culturally distinct from Aboriginal people on the mainland, and should be recognised. Thus, in 1989, Parliament changed the name to The Australian Institute of Aboriginal and Torres Strait Islander Studies (AIATSIS). Today, the designation 'Aboriginal' is avoided, but there has not been a call to rename the Institute once more, as The Australian Institute of Indigenous Studies or The Australian Institute of First Nation Studies (this would require a new Act of Parliament).
- The grammar of Walmatjari is far more complex than illustrated here. For instance, a modal root takes six sets of suffixes, indicating person and number of subject, object, indirect object, etc. Full details are in Hudson (1978).
- The pronoun system in Walmatjari is from Hudson (1978: 85) and that in Fitzroy Valley Kriol is from Hudson (1983: 44). Both sources quote a number of alternative forms. Sandefur (1979: 82–9) discusses the pronoun system in another dialect of Creole.
- Publications on Yidiñ are Dixon (1977, 1991).
- Schmidt (1985) provides an account of 'Young People's Dyirbal'; the traditional language is described in Dixon (1972).
- Langlois (2004) discusses the 'Teenage Pitjantjatjara' spoken at Areyonga; not all topics are covered (for instance, there is little on pronouns or demonstratives). Traditional Pitjantjatjara is described in Glass and Hackett (1970).

- When people in an Indigenous community speak both an original language and English, an English-modified version of the traditional language evolves. A different situation is found at places in the north where Creole is also spoken—there is then a blend of Creole, English and the original language (which may have some of its grammar re-organised in a novel manner). Accounts of such 'mixed languages' include O'Shannessy (2005, 2016) on 'Light Warlpiri', and McConvell and Meakins (2005) and Meakins (2011, 2016) on 'Gurindji Kriol'.
- Information on Tiwi from Lee (1987).

References

Alpher, Barry. 1991. *Yir-Yoront Lexicon: Sketch and dictionary of an Australian language*. Berlin: Mouton de Gruyter.

Bani, Ephraim, and Klokeid, Terry J. 1971. 'An outline of Mabuiag morphology'. Manuscript in the Australian Institute of Aboriginal Studies.

Beaglehole, J.C. 1955. Editor of *The Journals of Captain James Cook on His Voyages of Discovery: The voyage of the* Endeavour *1768–1771*. Cambridge: Cambridge University Press.

Bowern, Claire L. 2012. *A Grammar of Bardi*. Berlin: De Gruyter Mouton.

Brown, A.R. 1913. 'Three tribes of Western Australia', *Journal of the Royal Anthropological Institute of Great Britain and Ireland* 43: 143–94.

Churchill, Winston S. 1950. *The Second World War*, Vol. III, *The Grand Alliance*. London: Cassell.

Crosby, A.W. 1986. *Ecological Imperialism: The biological expansion of Europe, 900–1900*. Cambridge: Cambridge University Press.

Crowley, Terry. 1978. *The Middle Clarence Dialects of Bandjalang*. Canberra: Australian Institute of Aboriginal Studies.

Crowley, Terry, and Dixon, R.M.W. 1981. 'Tasmanian', pp. 394–421, in *Handbook of Australian Languages*, Vol. 2, edited by R.M.W. Dixon and Barry J. Blake. Canberra: Australia National University Press, and Amsterdam: John Benjamins.

Dampier, William. 1697. *A New Voyage Round the World*. London: James Knapton.

Dampier, William. 1703. *A Voyage to New Holland*. London: James Knapton.

Dench, Alan C. 1995. *Martuthunira: A language of the Pilbara region of Western Australia*. Canberra: Pacific Linguistics.

Dixon, R.M.W. 1972. *The Dyirbal Language of North Queensland*. Cambridge: Cambridge University Press.

Dixon, R.M.W. 1977. *A Grammar of Yidiñ*. Cambridge: Cambridge University Press.

Dixon, R.M.W. 1989. 'The Dyirbal kinship system', *Oceania* 59: 245–68.

Dixon, R.M.W. 1991. *Words of Our Country: Stories, place names and vocabulary in Yidiny, the Aboriginal language of the Cairns–Yarrabah region*. St Lucia: University of Queensland Press.

Dixon, R.M.W. 2002. *Australian Languages: Their nature and development*. Cambridge: Cambridge University Press.

Dixon, R.M.W. 2015. *Edible Gender, Mother-in-law Style, and Other Grammatical Wonders: Studies in Dyirbal, Yidiñ, and Warrgamay*. Oxford: Oxford University Press.

Dixon, R.M.W. 2016. *Are Some Languages Better than Others?* Oxford: Oxford University Press.

Dixon, R.M.W. and Koch, Grace. 1996. *Dyirbal Song Poetry: The oral literature of an Australian rainforest people*. St Lucia: University of Queensland Press.

Dixon, R.M.W., Ramson, W.S., and Thomas, Mandy. 1990. *Australian Aboriginal Words in English: Their origin and meaning*. Melbourne: Oxford University Press.

Dixon, R.M.W., Moore, Bruce, Ramson, W.S., and Thomas, Mandy. 2006. *Australian Aboriginal Words in English: Their origin and meaning*. 2nd edn. Melbourne: Oxford University Press.

Elkin, A.P. 1932. 'Social organization in the Kimberley Division, north-western Australia', *Oceania* 2: 296–333.

Elkin, A.P. 1935. 'Initiation in the Bard tribe, north-west Australia', *Journal and Proceedings of the Royal Society of New South Wales* 69: 190–208.

Elkin, A.P. 1937. 'The nature of Australian languages', *Oceania* 8: 127–69.

Evans, Nicholas and Wilkins, David. 2000. 'In the mind's ear: The semantic extension of perception verbs in Australian languages', *Language* 76: 546–92.

Glass, Aimee, and Hackett, Dorothy. 1970. *Pitjantjatjara Grammar: A tagmemic view of the Ngaanyatjara (Warburton Ranges) dialect.* Canberra: Australian Institute of Aboriginal Studies.

Goddard, Cliff. 1983. 'A semantically oriented grammar of the Yankunytjatjara dialect of the Western Desert language'. PhD thesis, Australian National University.

Gunson, Niel. 1974. Editor of *Australian Reminiscences and Papers of L.E. Threlkeld*, Vols 1 and 2. Canberra: Australian Institute of Aboriginal Studies.

Hale, K.L. 1966. 'Kinship reflections on syntax: Some Australian languages', *Word* 22: 318–24.

Hansen, K.C. 1984. 'Communicability of some Western Desert communalects', pp. 1–112 of *Work Papers of SIL-AAB*, Series B, number 11. Darwin: Summer Institute of Linguistics, Australian Aborigines Branch.

Haviland, John. 1974. 'A last look at Cook's Guugu Yimidhirr word list', *Oceania* 44: 216–32.

Haviland, John B. 1979a. 'Guugu Yimidhirr', pp. 26–180 of *Handbook of Australian Languages*, Vol. 1, edited by R.M.W. Dixon and Barry J. Blake. Canberra: Australia National University Press, and Amsterdam: John Benjamins.

Haviland, John B. 1979b. 'How to talk to your brother-in-law in Guugu Yimidhirr', pp. 161–239 of *Languages and Their Speakers*, edited by Timothy Shopen, Cambridge MA: Winthrop.

Haviland, John B. 1979c. 'Guugu Yimidhirr brother-in-law language', *Language in Society* 8: 365–93.

Haviland, John B. 1989. 'Guugu Yimidhirr dictionary'. Ms.

Heeres, J.E. 1899. *The Part Borne by the Dutch in the Discovery of Australia.* London: Luzac.

Hudson, Joyce. 1978. *The Core of Walmatjari Grammar.* Canberra: Australian Institute of Aboriginal Studies.

Hudson, Joyce. 1983. *Grammatical and Semantic Aspects of Fitzroy Valley Kriol*. Darwin: Summer Institute of Linguistics, Australian Aborigines Branch.

Jones, Phillip. 1996. *Boomerang: Behind an Australian icon*. Kent Town, South Australia: Wakefield Press.

King, Phillip P. 1827. *Narrative of a Survey of the Intertropical and Western Coasts of Australia Performed Between the Years 1818 and 1822*. London: John Murray.

Langlois, Annie. 2004. *Alive and Kicking: Areyonga teenage Pitjantjatjara*. Canberra: Pacific Linguistics.

Lee, Jennifer. 1987. *Tiwi Today: A study of language change in a contact situation*. Canberra: Pacific Linguistics.

McConvell, Patrick, and Meakins, Felicity. 2005. 'Gurindji Kriol: A mixed language emerges from code switching', *Australian Journal of Linguistics* 25: 9–30.

Meakins, Felicity. 2011. *Case Marking in Contact: The development and function of case morphology in Gurindji Kriol*. Amsterdam: John Benjamins.

Meakins, Felicity. 2016. 'No fixed address: The grammaticalisation of the Gurindji locative as a progressive suffix', pp. 367–95 of *Loss and Renewal: Australian languages since colonisation*, edited by Felicity Meakins and Carmel O'Shannessy. Berlin: De Gruyter Mouton.

Meggitt, M.J. 1962. *Desert People: A study of the Walbiri Aborigines of Central Australia*. Sydney: Allen & Unwin.

Morphy, Howard. 1977. '"Too many meanings": An analysis of the artistic system of the Yolngu of north-east Arnhem Land'. PhD thesis, Australian National University.

Mulvaney, D.J. 1989. *Encounters in Place: Outsiders and Aboriginal Australians 1606–1985*. St Lucia: University of Queensland Press.

Myers, Fred R. 1976. '"To have and to hold": A study of persistence and change in Pintupi social life'. PhD dissertation, Bryn Mawr.

O'Grady, Geoffrey N. 1966. 'Proto-Ngayarda phonology', *Oceanic Linguistics* 5: 73–139.

O'Shannessy, Carmel. 2005. 'Light Warlpiri: A new language', *Australian Journal of Linguistics* 25: 31–57.

O'Shannessy, Carmel. 2016. 'Entrenchment of Light Warlpiri morphology', pp. 217–51 of *Loss and Renewal: Australian languages since colonisation*, edited by Felicity Meakins and Carmel O'Shannessy. Berlin: De Gruyter Mouton.

Rumsey, Alan. 2000. 'Bunuba', pp. 34–153 of *The Handbook of Australian Languages*, Vol. 5, edited by R.M.W. Dixon and Barry J. Blake. Melbourne: Oxford University Press.

Sandefur, John R. 1979. *An Australian Creole in the Northern Territory: A description of the Ngukurr-Bamyili dialects (Part One)*. Darwin: Summer Institute of Linguistics, Australian Aborigines Branch.

Schmidt, Annette. 1985. *Young People's Dyirbal: An example of language death from Australia*. Cambridge: Cambridge University Press.

Sneddon, James N. 1996. *Indonesian Reference Grammar*. Sydney: Allen & Unwin.

Stokes, Bronwyn. 1982. 'A description of Nyigina, a language of the West Kimberley, Western Australia'. PhD thesis, Australian National University.

Tench, Watkin. 1979. *Sydney's First Four Years*. Sydney: Library of Australian History. [Reprint of 1789 original.]

Vogan, A.J. 1891. *The Black Police: A story of modern Australia*. London: Hutchinson.

Wodehouse, P.G. 1929. *Mr Mulliner Speaking*. London: Herbert Jenkins.

Index